Praise for *Taking Smart Risks*

"The risk-taking concepts in this book lie at the heart of effective leadership. Using case studies and stories from executives who've 'been there, done that,' Doug Sundheim teaches us that sometimes the most dangerous thing to do—in business and life—is to play it safe."

—Marshall Goldsmith, million-selling author of the New York Times bestsellers, *MOJO* and *What Got You Here Won't Get You There*

"In *Taking Smart Risks*, Doug Sundheim delivers a message that every business needs to hear right now; excessive risk will kill you, but so will complacency. In a highly approachable and no-nonsense style Sundheim spells out exactly what you need to do to get better at taking smart risks. If you're charged with driving growth in your organization, buy this book—but more importantly, use it."

—Jed Hartman, Group Publisher, Fortune & CNNMoney.com

"A spectacular book! The stories were powerful, the advice was crystal clear, and every few pages called me to action. I have bookmarked more pages in *Taking Smart Risks* than I have in any book since reading Peter Drucker's classics."

—Michael Hejtmanek, President & CEO, Hasselblad Bron Inc.

"Doug Sundheim does an excellent job of demonstrating not only how to take smart risks, but also how to lead the process of risk-taking; a critical skillset for leaders today."

—Cindy Zollinger, President & CEO, Cornerstone Research

A compelling case for why smart risk taking is so important in today's fast-paced, uncertain world."

—Willie Pietersen, Professor, Columbia Business School; Former CEO, Tropicana and Seagram USA

"*Taking Smart Risks* is engaging and challenging—exactly what a great business book should be. The ideas and tools that Doug Sundheim shares will significantly increase your chances of success when something important is on the line. They will also change how you think about and approach risk in every aspect of your life."

—Elizabeth Haas Edersheim, author of *The Definitive Drucker* and former McKinsey Partner

"A must-read for any Leader AND their teams . . . A powerful and practical guide for anyone looking to create new possibilities with greater confidence."

—Michael Hamilton, Partner, Chief Learning and Development Officer, Ernst & Young, Americas

"Organizational success or failure is not simply dependent on the ability to identify and avoid risk, but is also reliant on the ability to recognize and capitalize on fleeting opportunities through the use of smart-risk decisions. Using easy-to-follow examples and concrete advice, Doug Sundheim's book draws connections between the two, showing how any leader can get better at succeeding in times of uncertainty."

—Tom Zelibor, Rear Admiral (Ret.), U.S. Navy;
Director of Global Operations, U.S. Strategic Command

Taking Smart Risks is an invaluable resource for any successful person who wants to get even better. It is as intriguing as it is practical. Doug points out that risk taking is as much a game of emotions as it is a game of numbers. You need fire to get out of the gates, discipline to plan and act, and trust to build a strong team around you. *Taking Smart Risks* gives you tools to do all the above.

—Jack Beach, Manager of Leadership Strategy & Research, IBM;
Author, *Leadership in My Rearview Mirror:
Reflections from Vietnam, West Point, and IBM*

"With memorable stories and incisive logic, Sundheim not only makes a profoundly important argument for leaders in all sectors but also provides practical tools for navigating the tricky waters between unwisely excessive risk and dangerous complacency with the status quo. In today's turbulent waters more than ever, this is a must-read for leaders at all levels."

—Jeff Wetzler, EVP of Teacher Preparation, Support, and
Development, and Chief Learning Officer, Teach For America

"The risk-taking tools that Doug Sundheim shares are easy to understand and use in a real world context. I consider myself an intelligent risk taker and this framework has helped me and my team get even better.

—Joanna Rupp, Chief Operating Officer,
University of Chicago Office of Investments

"Most students begin my course assuming that good strategies *avoid* risk. Yet their future success–in both business and personal lives–depends on grasping the counterintuitive point that complacency is risky too. Doug's engaging style and relevant examples provide readers with access to advances in behavioral research, helping them to escape paralysis and develop into engines of positive change."

—David Souder, Assistant Professor of Management,
University of Connecticut School of Business

"The worst thing leaders can say to themselves is, 'why didn't I take that risk; why did I play it safe' . . . . only to fail!! Doug Sundheim's wonderful new book *Taking Smart Risks* goes a long way to helping understand why we make safe choices and how in the long run it only hurts us. His theories go against all that we have been taught by parents and even teachers, encouraging us to take the safe route. Doug Sundheim breaks those rules and in the end will set new rules for leaders of today. . . . and tomorrow!"

—Steven James, President of Manhattan Brokerage,
Prudential Douglas Elliman Real Estate

TAKING SMART RISKS

HOW SHARP LEADERS WIN
WHEN STAKES ARE HIGH

DOUG SUNDHEIM

New York   Chicago   San Francisco   Lisbon   London   Madrid   Mexico City
Milan   New Delhi   San Juan   Seoul   Singapore   Sydney   Toronto

The **McGraw·Hill** Companies

Copyright © 2013 by Doug Sundheim. All rights reserved. Printed in the United States of America. Except as permitted under the United States Copyright Act of 1976, no part of this publication may be reproduced or distributed in any form or by any means, or stored in a database or retrieval system, without the prior written permission of the publisher.

1 2 3 4 5 6 7 8 9 10   QFR/QFR   1 8 7 6 5 4 3 2

ISBN   978-0-07-177819-0
MHID   0-07-177819-5

e-ISBN   978-0-07-177820-6
e-MHID   0-07-177820-9

Library of Congress Cataloging-in-Publication Data

Sundheim, Doug.
    Taking smart risks:how sharp leaders win when stakes are high/by Doug Sundheim.
      p.   cm.
    ISBN 978-0-07-177819-0 (alk. paper)—ISBN 0-07-177819-5 (alk. paper)
    1. Risk management.   2. Leadership.   I. Title.
   HD61.S857   2013
   658.4'092—dc23   2012033523

McGraw-Hill books are available at special quantity discounts to use as premiums and sales promotions or for use in corporate training programs. To contact a representative, please e-mail us at bulksales@mcgraw-hill.com.

This book is printed on acid-free paper.

* * *

To my wife and sons,
Daryn, Eli, and Shai

* * *

CONTENTS

PART FOUR: ACT FAST, LEARN FAST

PART FIVE: COMMUNICATE POWERFULLY

PART SIX: CREATE A SMART-RISK CULTURE

FOREWORD

Think for a moment about your relationship to risk. Most of us never do, in any rational, systematic, ongoing way. Instead, we instinctively avoid risk wherever we can, only to occasionally and impulsively overindulge it, usually to no good end. Risk is built into every choice we make, but few of us know how to manage it to our advantage.

Then along comes Doug Sundheim, arguing in these pages that the answer lies in something called "smart risk,"—a paradoxical notion that significantly increases our odds of success in any given endeavor, he says, and can also make our lives richer and more vital.

In the 1960s, the psychologist Mihaly Csikszentmihalyi described the experience of "flow" as the sort of total immersion in an activity that generates a feeling of effortless energy, and well-being. Flow, he went on to say, lies somewhere between boredom and anxiety.

So does smart risk. Too little risk eventually prompts boredom, complacency, and, ultimately, atrophy. Too much risk, by contrast, prompts anxiety and ultimately leads to failure. Sundheim is interested in the territory in between—the "smart-risk zone"—where he argues the greatest learning, growth, and progress occur.

All my instincts tell me he's got this just right.

In large part, I know this from all the experiences I've had of living outside the smart-risk zone. On the one hand, some of my unhappiest times have been those I've spent squarely in my comfort zone, collecting a solid paycheck to do some job, but feeling trapped, stuck, and a bit stir crazy. At the other extreme, I can remember frightening times when I simply overreached and took stupid risks, ignoring the evidence that

I didn't have the skills necessary to accomplish the task I'd agreed to take on.

Using risk to our advantage, Sundheim says, begins with the mindset we bring to it. What he terms the "Paralysis Perception" is grounded in the fear-based question "What might I lose if I do this?" What he calls the "Power Perception" is grounded in the opposite inquiry: "What might I lose if I *don't* do this? If you're not moving forward, he concludes, you're probably moving backward.

At the heart of the capacity to take smart risks is genuine passion—or what Sundheim calls "Something Worth Fighting For." A "SWFF," he says, must be simple, stir emotion, lend itself to a story or narrative, and inspire action. The SWFF that worked for me in founding my own company at the age of 50 was the notion of "changing the way the world works"— meaning creating a new kind of workplace. It has proved galvanizing for me even in very tough times.

The necessary counterbalance to passion, Sundheim goes on to say, is the capacity to look into the future and predict the points at which you're at risk of failing and how you'll handle them should they occur. Far too many of us get derailed from taking smart risks by overly focusing on the immediate obstacles and insufficiently planning for future ones.

In this same spirit, a key to taking smart risks is to envision the worst-case scenario and ask yourself soberly, "Could I live with that?" For me, the worst-case scenario was that the business I had launched would fail, and I'd have to go back to journalism. I decided I could live with that, but, perhaps more important, asking the question made me realize I was prepared to considerably scale back the level at which I lived if that's what it took to persist in following my passion.

Counterintuitively, perhaps, much of this book is about learning how to live with failure—since it's both an inevitable by-product of taking risks and the reason that most of us are loathe to take them.

Smart risk takers, it turns out, learn how to embrace failure. "I missed more than 9,000 shots in my career," said Michael Jordan. Twenty-six times I was trusted to take the game-winning shot and missed. I've failed over and over and over again in my life. And that is why I succeed."

Sundheim's background is as a business consultant, and in that spirit he provides a slew of simple but powerful exercises to assess whether you're asking yourself the right question about any given decision. At the same time, he brings his theories to life with a range of real-life stories about business-people taking smart risks.

I'll never look at risk taking in the same way again after absorbing these insights. Neither will you.

—Tony Schwartz
CEO, The Energy Project and author of the bestsellers,
The Power of Full Engagement and *Be Excellent at Anything*

ACKNOWLEDGMENTS

It takes a village to raise a child, and the same can be said of publishing a book. Over the past three years, I've learned both lessons first-hand. Since starting my research and writing, my wife has given birth to both our sons. I had hoped to finish the book before the first was born, but it turned out I wasn't done until after the second arrived.

My deepest love and gratitude go to my wife, Daryn, for supporting my desire to write this book. At a time in our lives when she had every right to ask me to put this project on hold for five to ten years, she didn't. She knew how important it was to me. Between both of our careers, and with two new children, we somehow carved out enough time to let me write. Daryn also found time to provide feedback and input on my writing along the way. Her support redefined what love means to me.

Our families were a critical support system as well, often dropping whatever they had going on in their own lives to drive or fly to give us a hand. Ellen, thank you for practically moving in with us at a few particularly challenging points. Your help was invaluable. Thanks also to Morris, Dad, Pat, Mom, Tom, Jeff, Carrie, Nuno, and Karly for everything you've done and continue to do. Lixa, thank you for your wonderful care of our children.

With regard to the book itself, my mom, Pam Dodd, was instrumental in helping me get this final product finished. A PhD in organizational psychology, she was a tremendous thought partner and sounding board throughout. More than anyone, she listened to my daily frustrations about a particular concept or chapter that wasn't working, helping me find a new path or different idea. An excellent writer, she also took the first editing pass at each chapter, helping to tighten the language and flow. On many levels, I am where I am today because of her. Thanks, Mom.

Tony Schwartz was an advisor and role model since day one, giving input on everything from big conceptual ideas down to the tactical art of writing. An insightful and tireless critical thinker on the human condition, he provided new and helpful angles from which to think about risk taking. That also made him a natural to write the foreword. Thanks, Tony, for your time and friendship.

Thanks also to my agent, Alice Martell, for believing in this project at its earliest stages. Alice's passion, focus, and dedication were pivotal in helping me get over many hurdles. She's supportive and warm, yet direct and tough, all qualities I needed at different points along the way. I truly appreciate her partnership.

Thanks to my editors at McGraw-Hill, Leila Porteous and Zach Gajewski. Leila's early support helped get the project out of the gates and build momentum. Zach provided thoughtful guidance on all aspects of the manuscript and marketing, getting the book into its final polished form. Thanks also to McGraw-Hill publisher Mary Glenn for her support.

Others played consistently supportive roles throughout the process for which I'm grateful. My stepfather, Tom Connellan, a bestselling business author, shared his battle scars and hard-won lessons about writing and marketing books. Thanks for your support, Tom. My dad, Jim Sundheim, and sisters, Elizabeth and Kate, read early chapters and gave me the confidence that I had a solid concept to build on. Jeff Sundheim and Scott Sundheim, my uncle and brother, respectively, and both marketing executives, were excellent creative-thought partners. My cousin, Dan Sundheim, provided helpful access and insight into companies and risk taking with regard to investing. James Buchanan helped with research and story development. Jill Logan helped with project management as things got extremely chaotic toward the end. Jill also helped ensure that my consulting clients received top-notch service as I worked around the clock in the final two months. Deb Mills-Scofield opened her client list and gave of her time like an old friend even though we had just met. Jud Dean and Cassie Cone at DaVita were generous with their time and access to their team.

Many other clients, colleagues, and friends were generous in sharing stories and ideas, reading chapters, and providing feedback. I'm deeply appreciative of their support: Liz Edersheim, Omri Dahan, Tom Miller, Ana Maria Sencovici, Carl Petty, Sarah McGill, Jonathan Becker, Daniel Levitt, Jody Cornish, Jeff Wetzler, Andrew Deutscher, Michael Thomas, Annie Perrin, Bruce Schoenberg, Larry Tribble, Scotty Watson, Tom Zelibor, Mike Waite, Jono Steinberg, J. Parsons, Mike Latham, Matt Hlavin, Jennifer Palinchik, Richard Moross, Vivek Shah, David Richter, Vin Vacanti, Cyrus Massoumi, David Souder, Joe Moore, Jim Murphy, Charles Parry, Jack Beach, Jed Hartman, Bill Markel, Jason Bonadio, John Brunetti, Bob Solfanelli, Mike Hillyard, Patty Rose, Joanna Rupp, Lisa Anderson, Jenna McGraw, Rex Madden, Bruce Eckfeldt, Robert Glenn, Laura Lucas, Lyle Yorks, Steve Shulman, Mark Sanborn, Giff Constable, Steven Kotok, Bob McKinnon, and James Nawojchik. Thanks to you all.

PART ONE

REFRAMING RISK

The Dangers of Playing It Safe

Security is mostly a superstition. It does not exist in nature. . . . Avoiding danger is no safer in the long run than outright exposure.

—HELEN KELLER

When you think of someone who's playing it safe, you rarely think of a guy like Vivek Shah. By 2008, when he was 36 years old, Shah was group president, digital publishing at Time Inc. He was responsible for all online news, business, and sports properties, including Time.com, Life.com, SI.com, and CNNMoney.com. A creative thinker and change agent, Shah was promoted to group president because he had a knack for reinventing old magazine brands so that they could succeed in the new digital world. His biggest success was creating CNNMoney.com, a single consumer-friendly destination for all of Time's financial information that is now among the company's most valuable assets. He was named to *Crain's New York Business*'s prestigious 40 under 40 list in 2006 (top 40 businesspeople in New York under age 40), and many in the industry felt that Shah was on a fast track to becoming CEO of Time.

However, Shah felt he needed a change.

In early 2010, with a stellar track record and despite a bright future in front of him, Shah walked away from Time to buy

Ziff Davis, an ailing computer magazine publisher that was saddled with debt and just out of bankruptcy. He's the first to admit that it seemed like a crazy decision. But he had done his homework, and he had a vision for how to revive the once-storied brand. Finding backers, Shah crossed his fingers and jumped in. Two years later, having shed all print titles, rebuilt online brands, and launched a promising new data product, he's in full growth mode, and his prospects for the future look good.

When I asked Shah why he took the enormous career and financial risk of trying to bring Ziff Davis back from the dead, he said that beyond thinking it was a smart deal, he needed to prove something to himself.

"I had come to a point in my career where I wanted to know what I was made of," he said. "Staying at Time would have been the safe thing to do. But I wanted to know if I could build a business on my own. Could I take a risk outside of a large corporation and succeed? That question really bothered me. And I knew it would keep bothering me until I tried to answer it. The emotional cost of *not* risking and having to live with that regret was much greater in my mind than any career or financial costs I would incur."

In my work as a leadership and strategy consultant, this is a theme I hear often. Money is important, but a sense of accomplishment, growth, and self-knowledge is what really drives leaders, teams, and organizations to take risks.

When you play it safe, staying in the comfort zone for too long, you don't feel these things. You stagnate. And that puts everything at risk.

What It Means to Play It Safe

Playing it safe means that you've disengaged from meaningful challenges, aren't pushing yourself or your organization to grow, and aren't creating your future, but rather being passively dragged into it.

Shah's story illustrates how personal the definition of playing it safe is. Others in his situation might have considered the path to CEO to be all the challenge they needed. But that didn't matter to Shah because he didn't see it that way. Knowing himself and the questions he wanted to answer, he felt that he would be playing it safe if he stayed at Time and knew that he had to make the leap.

Over the past 60 years, professionals from the fields of psychology, philosophy, and adult development have recognized the need to engage in meaningful challenges as a primary driving force in living a satisfying life.[1] Whether you're rich or poor, young or old, you need to get out of your comfort zone regularly if you want to enjoy life. That's because the real reward for leaving your comfort zone never lies in what you achieve by doing it; it lies in the *process* of doing it. You become engaged and energized, clear and confident—in a word, alive.

Leaving your comfort zone fuels growth and development throughout life. It pushes you past perceived boundaries, allowing you to realize your potential. On one level, everyone knows this. We've all faced challenges, taken risks, and learned profound things about what we're capable of doing. We've felt invigorated. And we've inspired ourselves and others in the process.

Yet on another level, it's easy to forget these moments. Fooled into thinking that it's the end results, not the process of risk taking itself, that hold the primary value, we pull back and coast. We find comfort, and we don't want to lose it. We start playing it safe, ignoring the warning signs that this is a bad idea. We seem to forget that comfort is never permanent.

Shah spotted this pitfall and avoided it. Many people don't.

How We Miss the Warning Signs

The dangers of taking *too much* risk are very clear. We're reminded of them in the news every day. Businesses, families, and individuals are ruined in shocking fashion—"150-year-old bank and pillar of Wall Street is gone in the blink of an eye"; "Major oil company loses $90 billion in market value in three months"; "Kite surfer tries his luck in a hurricane and slams into a building." Astounding lapses in judgment are everywhere. The warnings of overambitious risks are clear—watch yourself and don't do anything stupid.

Unfortunately, we rarely hear any warnings about playing it safe. We don't see news headlines that say, "Low-risk approach forces local business to file for bankruptcy," or, "Stunningly conservative move pushes global pharmaceutical company to the brink of failure," or "Man retires after a mediocre career and feels painful remorse for never having laid anything on the line."

The dangers of playing it safe aren't sudden, obvious, and dramatic. They don't make headlines. They develop slowly over time and are almost impossible to pinpoint. This fact often makes them *more* dangerous than the high-profile missteps we see and hear about in the news because, like a slow leak in a tire, you don't see or feel these dangers on a daily basis. You become aware of them only when you realize that you're stuck and you're not really sure how it happened.

The dangers of playing it safe are hidden, silent killers. You miss a job opportunity, lose a sale, get beaten to market by a competitor, lose a star employee, or hurt a relationship. None of these signals that you might not be taking important risks is enough to set off alarms. Your defense mechanisms quickly step in to do damage control. You convince yourself and others that *it wasn't right for me anyway*, or *I didn't really want it*, or *the timing was bad*, or *I was busy with other things*. Then you go about your business as if nothing unusual has happened.

But somewhere in the back of your mind, you know that something is off. You're slipping a little. You're a step behind. You feel insecure. The walls you need to climb look higher and higher each day than they did the day before. You know you should be getting out there, taking action, and making changes. But you don't. You feel trapped.

You don't want to feel the regret of doing nothing, but you don't want to feel the pain of doing something stupid either. So you sit and play it safe, hoping that things will get better.

But they never do on their own.

The Five Dangers of Playing It Safe

As Shah mentioned in the opening story, the costs of *not* taking a risk are often much greater than the costs of taking it. When you take a risk, you might sacrifice comfort, time, or money. But when you don't take a risk, you sacrifice knowing yourself and feeling a sense of accomplishment.

In the early 1940s, renowned psychologist Abraham Maslow developed his now-famous hierarchy of needs to explain what motivates people.[2] At the bottom of the ladder are food and water for survival. At the top is the realization of your fullest potential. In between are varying levels of accomplishment.

One of the most profound insights from Maslow's research is that once basic survival needs are met, the act of climbing the ladder is more indicative of quality of life than reaching any particular rung. This means that you enjoy life more while you're moving from rung two to rung three than when you're just sitting on rung four, even though rung four is a higher level of achievement. You enjoy life more when you're pushing yourself and expanding your horizons. You can't climb Maslow's hierarchy by playing it safe.

Across a wide variety of clients, at both individual and organizational levels, I've seen five common dangers of playing it safe for too long.

- ▶ You don't win.
- ▶ You don't grow.
- ▶ You don't create.
- ▶ You lose confidence.
- ▶ You don't feel alive.

Unfortunately, these dangers tend to be like a row of dominoes. When one falls down, it sets off a chain reaction that takes the other ones with it, creating anything but comfort. It's only then that you realize that it would have been a lot less painful to just take risks in the first place.

Following are a few examples of how these dangers play out.

You Don't Win

When you play it safe for too long, you can forget what it feels like to win or, even worse, that winning is important to you at all. You feel off, but you may not be able to put your finger on exactly why. That's what happened to Alex.

Alex loved to win and had a track record to prove it. A senior account manager at a building products company, he had won some of the biggest accounts in his region over a 20-year period. Both his colleagues and his competitors considered him one of the most successful salespeople in his industry. But with success came a false sense of security.

Having a large list of steady buyers, Alex stopped putting time and effort into winning new business. He became less aggressive, less creative, and less focused. For 10 years, his numbers stayed strong, hiding the fact that he was half checked-out.

Then the market softened and many of his buyers lost their jobs. He hadn't spent much time building relationships with the junior buyers who took their place. Suddenly, Alex's numbers were cut in half. That put him in a position he'd never wanted to be in—having to hustle and pound the pavement the way he had done three decades earlier.

As he looked back, Alex regretted putting himself in that desperate position. But even more, he regretted having lost touch with a part of life he had enjoyed so much: the thrill of the hunt, taking on new challenges, and finding a way to win. While Alex had found the last 10 years comfortable, they hadn't really been rewarding.

You Don't Grow

Staying in the comfort zone is like standing still on a moving treadmill. You don't stay in the same spot; you move backward as you slowly lose your inclination to grow. If you want to keep moving forward, you have to take risks. Avi found this out the hard way.

A vice president of technology at a global bank, Avi thought he had the promotion to divisional senior vice president in the bag. He'd been with the company for more than 15 years, was one of its sharpest software architects, and was considered by almost everyone a shoo-in for the job. Yet he lost the promotion to a guy with less experience. Why? He never pushed himself to develop his client management skills.

Managing clients made Avi uncomfortable. He didn't feel that was where his real "value-add" was. After all, he was a computer programmer at heart. He loved developing software, not relationships. While Avi knew that client management was a big part of the SVP job, he thought his software skills would buy him a pass on relationship skills. He planned to learn what he'd need to know after he got the promotion.

That turned out to be a bad decision. Client management skills were a nonnegotiable prerequisite for the job, even for someone with Avi's technical expertise and reputation. Not pushing himself to grow when he needed to cost him the promotion.

You Don't Create

Progress is impossible without creation, and creation is impossible in the comfort zone. Julia realized this a few years too late.

Julia was a sharp management consultant who'd become a principal at a major consulting firm. By most people's measures, she was successful. But Julia dreamed of starting her own product company. When a former client with a good reputation approached her about joining him in a new venture in the beverage business, she thought it could be her shot.

For the next six months, Julia worked diligently with her former client on creating their company, forecasting revenues, sourcing suppliers, and analyzing distribution options. The business was looking promising.

When it finally came time for her to leave her consulting job to join the new business, however, she got a familiar knot in her stomach. It was the same feeling she'd had twice before when she'd considered leaving to start an entrepreneurial venture. "Stay put in your consulting job," it said. "Leaving is too risky." The irony was that Julia had been advising clients for years on how to take similar risks, but she couldn't find the courage to do it herself. She'd convinced herself that failure was inevitable. So she made the decision to pass on the beverage opportunity and stay in her current position.

Seven years later, her former client sold the beverage venture to another big player for $30 million. Julia was still working in management consulting, on the same types of projects, with the same people, at the same level. The risks of failing that Julia had worried about seven years earlier were tiny compared to the opportunities she'd actually lost to create something valuable of her own.

You Lose Confidence

We've all experienced losing confidence playing some kind of game. You're in the lead, but then you start losing a little. Panicking, you decide to play it safe, and you switch from playing to win to playing not to lose in order to preserve your lead. That's when the real trouble starts. You're not as aggressive as you were. You start losing more, you tighten up, and your confidence goes down the tubes. Jonathan experienced this in launching his company.

Jonathan was a successful software product manager who decided to strike out on his own. He had a good idea for an online HR software product, and he was confident that he could bring it to market successfully. He convinced several investors to back him.

A couple of years into the process, he lost two key $50,000 sales back to back. After that, he started second-guessing everything. Was he focusing on the right market? Did he have the right product? Did he have the right feature set? What was most damaging was that Jonathan began to believe that his competitors' products were superior to his.

Afraid to lose again, he stopped pursuing sales aggressively, opting instead to "perfect" his product first. But in so doing, he took himself out of the game, all but guaranteeing that he would continue his downward slide. With his confidence in a tailspin, his angel investors got frustrated. He felt caught in a vicious cycle. He wasn't taking action because he wasn't confident, yet he couldn't build his confidence because he wasn't taking action. Eventually he folded the company.

You Don't Feel Alive

Risk taking has a natural ebb and flow. You can't go full speed ahead all the time. Eventually you have to drop back to a lower gear, intentionally playing it safer for a short time. That becomes a problem, however, when you forget to rev the engines again and stay in low gear for too long. Scott's experience is a good example.

The CEO of a successful marketing agency in New York City, Scott had hired me to help plan for his company's growth. During one of our meetings, something was bothering him, but he couldn't put his finger on it. In a moment of exasperated candor, he mentioned that while things were generally good in his business, he hadn't felt really alive in years, and he wasn't sure what to do about it.

Wanting to be helpful, I asked, "When was the last time you felt really alive?" I hoped his answer would give us some clues as to what he'd lost and how to find it again.

Scott reflected for a moment and then told the story of how he'd started his agency 12 years earlier. He walked me through his initial hesitancy and fear, the leap of faith and decision to move forward, the struggles in the first year after losing his cornerstone client, and the feeling of exhilaration at achieving his first $1 million in billings. He said he was proud of the company he'd created and felt that it was one of the greatest learning experiences of his life.

When he was done 15 minutes later, he had a big grin on his face.

"You look alive now!" I said.

"You're right." He laughed. "A minute ago, you asked me about my goals for the next year. I'd like to change my answer. I want that *feeling* back again."

That conversation became the foundation of our work together over the next year.

Since I stumbled upon that question more than 10 years ago with Scott, I've asked it of thousands of other people, "When did you last feel really alive?" Everyone's answer is different, but one thing is always the same: they felt the most alive when they were taking a meaningful risk, getting out of their comfort zones. Some were big risks; some were small. Some were personal risks; some were professional. Regardless, all were stretches. All contained the DNA of where and how to find satisfaction in life and feel truly alive.

Are You Caught in the Comfort Zone?

Here are the clues.

You're caught if you've reached a wall and don't take action to get past it. You're caught if you find yourself saying, "I have to do something here, but I don't know what," and yet you're not experimenting to figure it out.

Being caught in the comfort zone doesn't mean that you're sitting around doing nothing. It's more nuanced than that. You could be making progress, but not quickly enough. You could be taking chances, but not boldly enough. You could be going out on a limb, but not far enough, and the extra push is what will make a difference.

Perhaps you're caught in one part of your life, but not in another. Perhaps you've taken risks in the past, so you don't think of yourself as someone who hangs out in the comfort zone, yet you haven't taken any risks recently, and so currently you're caught. What counts is now, the present moment. Ultimately what counts the most for your growth and quality of life is figuring out how to get out of your comfort zone on a regular basis.

Getting Out of Your Comfort Zone

Just because you want to take risks doesn't mean it's easy to do. There's a chasm between knowing that you want to and actually doing it. Taking the first steps can feel awkward, difficult, and uncertain. It's easy to allow yourself to be overcome with concern or fear and get stuck, wishing that the situation were different but doing nothing about it.

The idea for this book grew out of listening to my clients—mainly leaders in large companies—say that they wanted their people to take more risks, yet not being able to articulate what that really meant. It got me thinking. How could I encapsulate smart risk taking to develop clear mindsets and actions to support my clients, as well as anyone who wanted to take more risks? The chapters that follow are the result of my exploration of the topic over the last decade. Included are stories of how others have approached risk taking intelligently and specific tools to help you do the same.

Chapter 1 Summary

▶ Even the most successful among us can get lulled into a comfort zone and get stuck playing it safe without realizing it.

▶ Often you miss the signs of playing it safe because you don't consider doing so to be dangerous. The negative effects take time to show up. As with a slow leak in a car tire, your energy and aliveness drain away little by little until one day you're completely deflated and you don't know how it happened.

▶ The dangers of playing it safe are significant. You don't win, don't grow, don't create, lose confidence, and don't feel alive.

▶ Being caught in the comfort zone doesn't necessarily mean sitting around doing nothing. You could be very active and still not be taking risks on the things that matter most to you.

▶ It's easy to want to get out of the comfort zone and yet do nothing about it. This book provides stories of others who've gotten out of their comfort zones and practical tools for you to learn how to get out of your own.

Shifting Your Perception of Risk—The Smart-Risk Zone

There are risks and costs to a program of action. But they are far less than the long-range risks and costs of comfortable inaction.

—JOHN F. KENNEDY

One reason we get caught in the comfort zone is that we don't see a viable alternative to it. We want to get out, but everything outside of the comfort zone looks dangerous. We may rationally know that this is not true; however, the *perception* of a danger zone looms large enough to stop us. If we don't do anything to shift that perception, we're left with two unattractive options: play it safe or lose control. We have no access to growth.

But if we take steps to shift our perception of danger, we can create a third zone, which I call the smart-risk zone. The smart-risk zone is characterized by an understanding that to drive growth, we have to find the middle ground between comfort and danger.

Seeing Only Comfort and Danger

Jessica Goldstein was a newly minted associate partner at PARA, a global operations consulting firm where she had worked for 15 years (names have been changed in this story). Long frustrated that the firm's solutions tended to stall during execution, Goldstein felt that the firm needed a new service: leadership consulting that would help clients implement changes. If successful, the service would improve client results and add a new revenue stream for PARA—not to mention that it could be a great project to help Goldstein increase her visibility within the partner ranks, a win-win-win.

Framing out her high-level thoughts, Goldstein shared the concept with her partners in the L.A. office. They agreed that the service offering had potential and that it could complement their projects. Jim Dorsten, a respected senior partner, went so far as to say that he thought the service could become a defining competitive advantage for PARA. They all agreed that it was worth further exploration.

Taking the positive cue, Goldstein reached out to PARA partners in other offices and engaged external leadership experts to help her understand the best next steps. What in-house capabilities to deliver leadership consulting did PARA already have? Where would the firm need to bring in external help? Which project would provide the best opportunity to pilot the service?

As she dug into these questions, she realized that developing the service would be trickier than she had anticipated. For it to succeed, leadership experts would need to be integrated into projects from the outset, not tacked on at the end; this added another layer of complexity to already complex engagements. Also, clients would need to be convinced that the service had real value; they didn't consider leadership consulting to be PARA's core strength. Finally, Avina Jain, a mentor and another senior partner, warned Goldstein that by pursuing this concept, she risked diverting her attention from the firm's core operational services. Jain agreed that the leadership offering could become a competitive advantage for PARA, but she also felt that the effort required to get it to that point could become a black hole for Goldstein, jeopardizing her career if she wasn't careful.

Unsure of how to proceed, Goldstein decided to stop driving the idea forward until she had a stronger sense that she could successfully spearhead the effort. Two years later, she hadn't taken any additional action.

I hear stories like Goldstein's all the time. Someone has a solid idea, but he freezes when it comes to getting out of the starting gate with it. He gets stuck between thinking that he has a good idea and worrying that he won't be able to pull it off. The situation usually plays out in this fashion:

1. See a possibility, perhaps a new opportunity or creative idea, and feel inspired.
2. Put some ideas together regarding how to pursue it.
3. Make a few "toe in the water" attempts to move it forward.
4. Quickly realize that it will be more difficult to achieve than initially thought.
5. Begin sweating at the thought of full-on pursuit and possible pitfalls.
6. Stop pursuing it and offer a plausible explanation for why stopping was the smartest thing to do
7. Commit to reengage when the circumstances look less risky.
8. Never find less risky circumstances.

There's a good reason that people never find less risky circumstances: they don't exist. Life is a series of one "not-quite-right" moment after another. Moving forward despite drawbacks is the only way to seize opportunity. Creation requires taking risks.

What Does It Mean to Risk?

I've always hated the dictionary definition of risk, "exposing oneself to the possibility of loss or injury." It presents only the downside. People who choose to take risks never frame it that way in their minds. How could they? If they did, they'd never take risks in the first place. Just imagine the following conversation.

"Hey, Doug, what did you do to make that project so successful?"

"Well, Tom, I was struggling at first, but then I exposed myself to the possibility of loss or injury and everything just started to fall into place."

"That sounds like a smart strategy, Doug—and a lot of fun! I think I'll try it."

Not a very likely conversation.

A more accurate definition of risk provides an upside to balance the possibility of loss. Any viable understanding of risk includes something that you can get excited about, something that makes the discomfort or danger worthwhile and reflects what's really at stake, both good and bad. Taking a risk then becomes "exposing oneself to the possibility of loss or injury *in the hopes of achieving a gain or reward*." That's much more descriptive of what's going on when you take a risk, and much more useful.

But even this more accurate definition is a little too sterile for what risk taking really entails. It gives the impression that deciding to take a risk involves a straightforward two-sided cost-benefit analysis. It's as if you load an imaginary scale with possible benefits on one side and possible costs on the other. If the benefits outweigh the costs, you take the risk. If the costs outweigh the benefits, you don't.

But risk taking is never that neat and clean. In real life, it's much messier than that. To illustrate, you could imagine the following dialogue running through Goldstein's head as she considers pursuing the leadership consulting business.

"I'm pretty clear that providing leadership consulting services is a good business idea. I've looked at it from several angles. However, I'm not 100 percent positive, and I'm also not sure that I can pull it off successfully. What happens if I pursue it and I fail? It could hurt my reputation. That would be a disaster. I don't want to lose the career I've worked so hard to build. I should run the idea by more people. Wait, I've already run it by a lot of people. Maybe I'm just blowing this possibility of failure out of proportion. On the other hand, maybe my hesitancy is my intuition telling me that the timing isn't right. Oh, I should stop being such a coward. Other people have done things like this and succeeded. Why not me? I'll tell you why not, because I'm not a risk taker. Then again, the other people weren't really necessarily big risk takers either. You know, the more I think about this, the fuzzier it gets. I have no idea what to do. I should get back to the project I was working on."

All of us have been in this muddled space. Tons of thoughts get mushed together in our mind: what we want; what we think we can achieve; what will be best for us; what will be best for our family; what we're rationally afraid of; what we're irrationally afraid of. Before we know it, our head is spinning. What seemed clear at first no longer does. We're not sure where to direct our focus.

Choosing the Right Focus for Risk Taking

Whether or not we take a risk in a given situation depends, in large part, on where we focus our attention as we weigh the pros and cons. If we focus on the upside of risk taking, we'll feel pulled to take the risk. If we focus on the downside, we'll feel pushed not to take the risk.

Unfortunately, our focus isn't derived from a rationally selected set of data. When we're making choices, we are all dealing with cognitive biases—ways in which our minds selectively pick out only certain pieces of information to pay attention to. One bias in particular has a significant impact on risk taking.

In the late 1970s two cognitive psychologists, Daniel Kahneman and Amos Tversky, employed a series of simple choice experiments in order to understand idiosyncrasies in the way people make decisions under uncertainty.[1] Their research uncovered what they called the loss-aversion bias. Put simply, they found that human beings hate to lose. We hate to lose so much that we'll do just about anything to avoid it, regardless of whether or not our actions are in our best interest.

To illustrate the loss-aversion bias, consider the following example.

Imagine that you're a doctor who's in charge of distributing a vaccine during a serious flu epidemic in which 600 people have become ill. You're faced with a choice between the following two programs:

> Program A: 200 lives will be saved.
>
> Program B: There is a one-third probability that 600 people will be saved and a two-thirds probability that no one will be saved.

Which do you choose? (Pick one before reading on.)

Now imagine that you're that same doctor during the same epidemic, but this time you have a different choice of programs:

> Program C: 400 people will die.
>
> Program D: There is a one-third probability that no one will die and a two-thirds probability that 600 people will die.

Which do you choose? (Pick one before reading on.)

You might already have figured out that the two sets of choices are the exact same options, presented differently. Kahneman and Tversky presented these exact scenarios to two groups of 150 doctors. One group had to chose between Programs A and B, and the other group had to choose between Programs C and D (unlike you, they didn't have the advantage of seeing both pairs together). The results were astonishing.

> In Group 1: 72 percent chose A (*avoid risk*) and 28 percent chose B (*take risk*).
>
> In Group 2: 22 percent chose C (*avoid risk*) and 78 percent chose D (*take risk*).

How could that be? Programs A and C were exactly the same, and so were Programs B and D. Why were the results so drastically different? Why did 75 percent of the doctors want to avoid taking the risk in the first scenario, yet 75 percent wanted to take the risk in the second?

The answer lies in how the information was framed to focus the doctors' attention. More specifically, it lies in how the possible *loss* was framed, which Kahneman and Tversky found is the strongest motivator of behavior under uncertainty.

The first group of doctors was focused on a *sure gain*— 200 lives saved. Loss-aversion bias made them *less* inclined to take a risk because they didn't want to lose those 200 lives. A doctor might think, "Why would I risk losing 200 people when I know I can definitely save them? That seems irresponsible."

Conversely, the second group of doctors was focused on a *sure loss*—400 people will die. Loss-aversion bias made them *more* inclined to take a risk because they didn't want to lose those 400 lives. In this case, a doctor might think, "How can I let those 400 people die without at least trying to save them? That seems irresponsible."

Ironically, both groups of doctors had the same goal— to save lives and avoid losses. Yet because their attention was focused differently, it led them to make very different decisions.

So, what are the implications of this insight for daily life?

> We choose where to focus our attention every day,
> *and*
> **WHERE we choose to focus our attention matters—**
> *big time.*

When you choose to focus on what you might lose by taking risks—that is, what you already have (like the first group of doctors)—it makes risk taking seem like a bad idea. When you choose to focus on what you might lose by *not* taking risks—that is, what you *don't* already have (like the second group of doctors)—it makes risk taking look like a smart idea.

To illustrate, consider what Goldstein from the earlier story could have been thinking from each focus, taking risk versus avoiding risk (see Table 2.1).

In both cases, loss aversion is at work. Goldstein is just worried about losing different things in each. Neither focus is right or wrong. They're merely choices based on situational assessments. There are times in life when failure would have disastrous consequences and risk taking *isn't* smart. And there are times when you need to go out on a limb and risk taking *is* smart. Keeping a balanced focus on the costs of both *taking* and *not taking* risks is how you distinguish between the two.

Of course, keeping that balanced focus isn't always easy. We're naturally more averse to the costs of taking risks than

TABLE 2.1   TAKING RISK VERSUS AVOIDING RISK

Focus	What Goldstein Might Be Thinking
LOSS FROM TAKING RISK	
Focusing on what she might lose by taking the risk . . .	My life is comfortable right now. I just got promoted. I'm good at what I do, and I've worked hard to get where I am. Also, I make good money, and my work's not terribly stressful.
. . . makes taking the risk seem like a bad idea.	I'm not sure it's worth disrupting this good thing that I've got. What if the new service doesn't work out? At best, I will have expended a lot of energy; at worst, I may have damaged my reputation at PARA.
LOSS FROM AVOIDING RISK	
Focusing on what she might lose by not taking the risk . . .	I haven't felt a real sense of accomplishment and engagement in several years. I miss that. Not to mention, I've never really put my stamp on anything around here. I want to do something I can look back on and feel really proud of.
. . . makes taking the risk seem like a good idea.	I'm going to have to step out a little and take some chances if I want to get to the next level of my career and feel energized about it. If I don't, I fear that I'll get into a rut that will be tough to get out of.

to those of *not* taking risks because of the time frames in which we experience each cost.

We experience the costs of *taking risks* immediately. Discomfort and uncertainty show up as soon as we engage in the risk. It's a bitter pill to swallow up front in the hopes of a possible, but not guaranteed, benefit down the road. Conversely, we experience the costs of *avoiding risks* further in the future. Low growth, lack of accomplishment, and limited fulfillment take time to manifest. Because these things are not immediately in front of us (and because they're less visceral than the costs of taking risks), we're less averse to them. In short, we have more trouble imagining what a lack of accomplishment will feel like in five years than what discomfort will feel like in five hours.

However, if we take the time to truly account for the long-term losses we incur by avoiding risks, removing them from the vague fog of the future, we can more deeply appreciate the consequences of *not* taking risks. They too can become a powerful motivator. The four-box cost-benefit analysis at the end of the chapter is a useful tool to help create a balanced view.

The Paralysis and Power Perceptions

Depending on the losses you choose to focus on when you're considering a risk, you create different realities for yourself. Two of these realities I call the *paralysis perception* and the *power perception.*

The paralysis perception is the result of focusing too much on the losses from taking risks (certainty, comfort, and control). It makes everything outside the comfort zone look dangerous. When discomfort and disaster are dominating your thinking, you take little, if any, risk (Figure 2.1). A common thought in the paralysis perception is, "Things may not be perfect now, but they're not that bad. If I make a move, things could end up worse. I'd better not risk it."

The power perception is the result of a balanced focus on the losses from both taking risks and *not* taking risks (loss

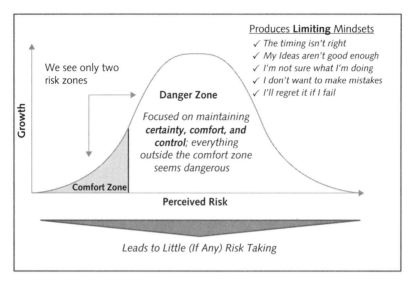

FIGURE 2.1   THE PARALYSIS PERCEPTION

of certainty, comfort, and control versus loss of growth, progress, and learning). Both opportunity and possibility dominate your thinking, shifting your perception of risk and enabling you to find the smart-risk zone (Figure 2.2).

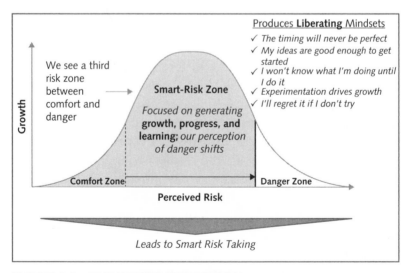

FIGURE 2.2   THE POWER PERCEPTION

A common refrain in the power perception is, "I'll regret it if I don't pursue this thing. I've got to find some smart ways to take risks to move it forward."

Helping you make the shift from paralysis to power is the purpose of this book.

The paralysis and power perceptions each produce a different group of mindsets that drive behavior. The paralysis perception produces limiting mindsets that discourage action and keep you stuck. The power perception produces liberating mindsets that encourage experimentation and keep you open to possibility. The more time you spend in the power perception, focused on growth, progress, and learning, the more you're able to hold the liberating mindsets required to take smart risks. This mindset shift from paralysis to power is represented in Table 2.2.

Note that the shifts aren't opposites. While the limiting mindsets reflect insecurity about moving forward—for example, "The timing isn't right," or, "My ideas aren't good enough"—the liberating mindsets don't reflect a higher degree of security than the limiting mindsets. It's not as if you shift from thinking that the timing isn't right to all of a sudden thinking that it is right—you merely accept that the timing will never be perfect. Nor do you shift from thinking that you

TABLE 2.2   FOCUSING ON A DESIRE TO GROW, PROGRESS, AND LEARN SHIFTS YOUR MINDSETS

From:		*To:*
LIMITING MINDSETS OF THE PARALYSIS PERCEPTION		**LIBERATING MINDSETS OF THE POWER PERCEPTION**
❏ The timing isn't right	⟹	❏ The timing will never be perfect
❏ My ideas aren't good enough	⟹	❏ My ideas are good enough to get started
❏ I'm not sure what I'm doing	⟹	❏ I won't know what I'm doing until I do it
❏ I don't want to make mistakes	⟹	❏ Experimentation drives growth
❏ I'll regret it if I fail	⟹	❏ I'll regret if if I don't try

don't know what you're doing to all of a sudden thinking that you do—you accept that you won't know what you're doing until you do it.

So instead of being a move from insecurity to security, the shift from limiting to liberating is more accurately a move from *needing* total security before moving forward to *understanding that you can't have* total security before moving forward. Liberating mindsets reflect an increase in your tolerance for uncertain circumstances. You realize that whatever pinch you'll feel from taking smart risks in the short term will usually be negligible compared to the pain you'll feel from avoiding them in the long term. This is the essence of the smart-risk zone. It's the result of coming to grips with the nature of growth and progress as inherently uncertain. Expecting and wanting it to be anything else is what creates paralysis.

This is the realization that Jessica Goldstein finally had. Creating the leadership consulting business had some inherent uncertainty in it, and moving it forward was going to take some risks no matter how she looked at it. She had to be OK with a degree of uncertainty before she could put a plan in place to take action and bring the service to market, which she eventually did several years later.

The following section, "Ideas and Tools for Action," is included in most chapters in the book. It contains exercises that are either referred to in the chapter or that I've used with clients to address the challenges that were discussed. Some tools and exercises might take you 10 minutes of individual reflection. Others might take as much as several months if you fold them into a planning process. The exercises will help elucidate key points; however, you do not need to do them to maintain continuity between chapters. My recommendation is that you skim through the tools as you read the chapters so that, even if you don't use them now, you can take a mental snapshot of how you might use them in the future.

Included here is a detailed cost-benefit analysis I used with Jessica Goldstein and instructions for how to do your own.

IDEAS AND TOOLS FOR ACTION

Four-Box Cost-Benefit Analysis

The four-box cost-benefit analysis is a good tool to help you see the costs and benefits of both taking and *not* taking a risk. While it may seem that the costs of one are merely the benefits of the other, that's not actually the case, as you'll see in the example that follows.

I developed this tool as a simple way to help clients uncover what psychologists call a *secondary gain*: the benefit we get from avoiding the very thing we say we want. Uncovering this balanced set of data puts you in a better position to take the right risks.

Before you do your own four-box analysis, let's look at an example to kick-start your thinking. This is Jessica Goldstein's actual analysis that helped her move forward with her plans for the leadership consulting business. Don't worry about the scoring. That will be explained when you do your own analysis. For now, I just want you to understand the types of things that go into each of the boxes.

In Figure 2.3, you'll see four separate, yet interconnected brainstorms that Goldstein did: the benefits of taking the risk, the costs of taking the risk, the benefits of avoiding the risk, and the costs of avoiding the risk.

Going through the process of doing a four-box cost-benefit analysis tends to make a few things clear. First, doing all four boxes is essential. Reflecting on each area individually tends to trigger different types of thinking, exposing the important richness and inherent "messiness" that need to be taken into account as you consider your decision.

For instance, one of Goldstein's benefits from taking the risk was that she'd be more marketable. However, the opposite of that ("I won't be marketable") didn't show up in the costs of avoiding the risk—nor did anything like it. Similarly, one of her costs of avoiding the risk was that she would never know if she had "what it takes" to make the new business a success if she didn't give it a try.

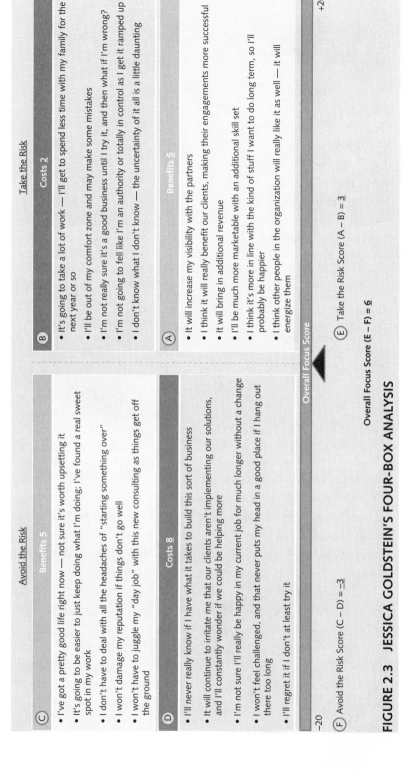

Avoid the Risk

C Benefits 5

- I've got a pretty good life right now — not sure it's worth upsetting it
- It's going to be easier to just keep doing what I'm doing; I've found a real sweet spot in my work
- I don't have to deal with all the headaches of "starting something over"
- I won't damage my reputation if things don't go well
- I won't have to juggle my "day job" with this new consulting as things get off the ground

D Costs 8

- I'll never really know if I have what it takes to build this sort of business
- It will continue to irritate me that our clients aren't implementing our solutions, and I'll constantly wonder if we could be helping more
- I'm not sure I'll really be happy in my current job for much longer without a change
- I won't feel challenged, and that never puts my head in a good place if I hang out there too long
- I'll regret it if I don't at least try it

Take the Risk

B Costs 2

- It's going to take a lot of work — I'll get to spend less time with my family for the next year or so
- I'll be out of my comfort zone and may make some mistakes
- I'm not really sure it's a good business until I try it, and then what if I'm wrong?
- I'm not going to fell like I'm an authority or totally in control as I get it ramped up
- I don't know what I don't know — the uncertainty of it all is a little daunting

A Benefits 5

- It will increase my visibility with the partners
- I think it will really benefit our clients, making their engagements more successful
- It will bring in additional revenue
- I'll be much more marketable with an additional skill set
- I think it's more in line with the kind of stuff I want to do long term, so I'll probably be happier
- I think other people in the organization will really like it as well — it will energize them

Overall Focus Score

−20   +20

Ⓕ Avoid the Risk Score (C − D) = −3   Ⓔ Take the Risk Score (A − B) = 3

Overall Focus Score (E − F) = 6

FIGURE 2.3   JESSICA GOLDSTEIN'S FOUR-BOX ANALYSIS

Self-knowledge and confidence didn't show up as explicitly in the benefits of taking the risk. Reflecting on all four areas offered her a more comprehensive set of insights.

Second, the four boxes force you to think in both the short and the long term, giving a more balanced view of the situation (see Figure 2.4).

The top two boxes tend to be focused on the short term, showing you what you'll get immediately with each choice. They make avoiding the risk more attractive. The bottom two boxes tend to be focused on the long term, pointing out what you'll get in the long run with each choice. They make taking the risk more attractive. The top boxes are indicative of the paralysis perception, while the bottom boxes are indicative of the power perception.

The upshot? Too much short-term focus leads to paralysis.

That's why Box D is critically important in these analyses. It's often a deciding factor in turning paralysis into power because it brings future costs into the present. Jessica Goldstein's situation is a great example. Her initial cost-benefit analysis was two-sided—the contents of Boxes A and C. In essence, she gave 5 points to each, leaving her with a focus score of zero—on the fence. The net effect was two years of paralysis. It wasn't until she reflected on the costs in Box D, giving that box a score of 8, that she was able to shift her perception from paralysis to power. Ultimately, this is what spurred her to action.

Instructions for the Four-Box Cost-Benefit Analysis

1. Think of a specific area where you want to make more progress, but you haven't because it feels too risky. It can be a project, challenge, or issue at work or in your personal life. It should be something that's meaningful, would excite you to achieve it, and is a stretch for you.

2. With regard to this risk, fill out Boxes A to D on the four-box model in Figure 2.5 (or re-create one on a separate sheet of paper).

   A. What are the benefits of taking the risk?

   B. What are the costs of taking the risk?

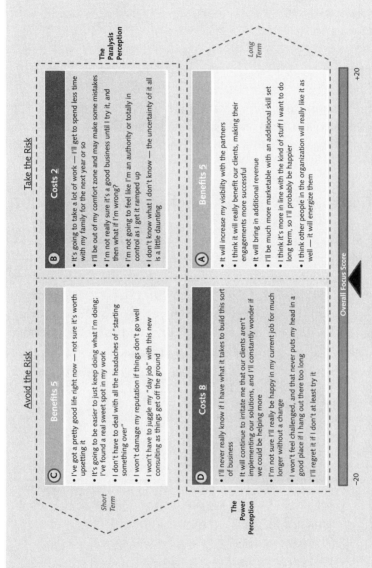

Avoid the Risk

Take the Risk

C Benefits 5

- I've got a pretty good life right now — not sure it's worth upsetting it
- It's going to be easier to just keep doing what I'm doing; I've found a real sweet spot in my work
- I don't have to deal with all the headaches of "starting something over"
- I won't damage my reputation if things don't go well
- I won't have to juggle my "day job" with this new consulting as things get off the ground

B Costs 2

- It's going to take a lot of work — I'll get to spend less time with my family for the next year or so
- I'll be out of my comfort zone and may make some mistakes
- I'm not really sure it's a good business until I try it, and then what if I'm wrong?
- I'm not going to feel like I'm an authority or totally in control as I get it ramped up
- I don't know what I don't know — the uncertainty of it all is a little daunting

The **Paralysis Perception**

Short Term

D Costs 8

- I'll never really know if I have what it takes to build this sort of business
- It will continue to irritate me that our clients aren't implementing our solutions, and I'll constantly wonder if we could be helping more
- I'm not sure I'll really be happy in my current job for much longer without a change
- I won't feel challenged, and that never puts my head in a good place if I hang out there too long
- I'll regret it if I don't at least try it

The **Power Perception**

A Benefits 5

- It will increase my visibility with the partners
- I think it will really benefit our clients, making their engagements more successful
- It will bring in additional revenue
- I'll be much more marketable with an additional skill set
- I think it's more in line with the kind of stuff I want to do long term, so I'll probably be happier
- I think other people in the organization will really like it as well — it will energize them

Long Term

−20   Overall Focus Score   +20

FIGURE 2.4   JESSICA GOLDSTEIN'S FOUR-BOX ANALYSIS, CONTINUED

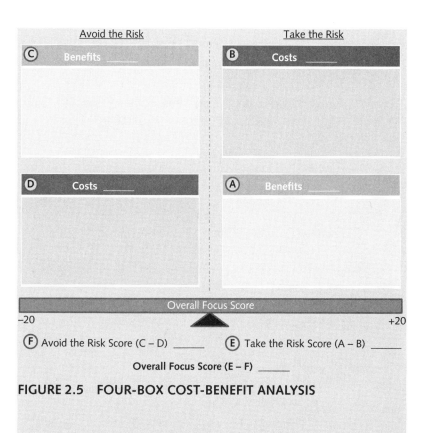

FIGURE 2.5   FOUR-BOX COST-BENEFIT ANALYSIS

C. What are the benefits of avoiding the risk?
D. What are the costs of avoiding the risk?
As you write your responses for each cost or benefit, make sure to include not only the outcomes *but also the emotion of how it feels. The more specific you are, the more valuable the exercise will be.*

3. Allocate points to the *benefits*
   ▶ Allocate 10 points between Boxes A and C based on the following question: *How important to me are these benefits?*
   ▶ The total must add up to 10 (for example, if you give 6 points to A, you must give 4 points to C).
   ▶ Write each allocation in the line next to benefits:
     A. _____
     C. _____

4. Allocate points to the *costs*:
   ▶ Allocate 10 points between Boxes B and D based on the following question: *How afraid am I of these costs?*
   ▶ Again, the total for the two must add up to 10.
   ▶ Write each allocation in the line next to costs:
      B. _____
      D. _____
5. Subtract costs from benefits in vertical columns.
   ▶ A _____ – B _____ = E _____ Take the risk score.
   ▶ C _____ – D _____ = F _____ Avoid the risk score.
   (Be careful to subtract the right numbers. It's normal to end up with negative numbers.)
6. Subtract the *avoid the risk* score from the *take the risk* score to get your focus score:
   ▶ E _____ – F _____ = G _____ Focus score.

Scoring Key

	Focus Score	What Your Focus Score Means with Regard to the Specific Area You Chose
Power Perception	+16 to +20	You thrive on taking risks and show little to no concern regarding downsides. This may be because what others consider downsides, you do not.
	+10 to +14	You see far greater value in taking the identified risks than in avoiding them. While you're aware of possible downsides to taking the risks, they seem small compared to the downsides of not taking them.
	+4 to +8	You see more value in taking the identified risks than in avoiding them; however, you're keenly aware of possible downsides and are likely to take a measured approach.
On the Fence (*net effect of paralysis*)	–2 to +2	You're on the fence as to whether or not you should take the risks; you perceive both the upsides and the downsides fairly evenly.

	Focus Score	What Your Focus Score Means with Regard to the Specific Area You Chose
Paralysis Perception	−4 to −8	You see more value in avoiding the identified risks than in taking them; however, you're keenly aware of the possible upsides and are likely to keep the idea of taking risks in the back of your mind.
	−10 to −14	You see far greater value in avoiding the identified risks than in taking them. While you're aware of possible upsides to taking the risks, they seem small compared to the upsides of not taking them.
	−16 to −20	You see little to no value in taking risks. This may be because what others consider upsides, you do not.

Chapter 2 Summary

▶ People often have important ideas but get stuck in the starting gate when they try to make them happen. The feeling of being stuck in the starting gate usually comes in a similar progression and ends in paralysis.

▶ The dictionary definition of risking is exposing yourself to loss or injury, but that's an incomplete definition. A more accurate definition of risk provides an upside that motivates us to take the risk in the first place.

▶ One reason we don't take risks has to do with the loss-aversion bias. We hate to lose. However, the loss-aversion bias can also explain why we *should* take risks because we can also lose a lot by avoiding risks. Your actions are determined by where you choose to focus.

▶ Depending on where you focus when you take risks, you create a different reality in which to live. Two such realities are the paralysis perception and the power perception.

▶ The paralysis perception is the result of focusing too much on the downside of taking risks. The power perception is the result of a balanced focus on the downside of both taking risks and *not* taking risks.

▶ The paralysis and power perceptions each produce a different group of mindsets that drive behavior, limiting and liberating mindsets, respectively. The more time we spend in the power perception, focused on growth, progress, and learning, the more we're able to hold the liberating mindsets required to take smart risks.

▶ The four-box cost-benefit analysis is a helpful tool for understanding the consequences of taking or avoiding risks in both the short term and the long term.

Smart Risk Taking

Take calculated risks. That is quite different from being rash.

—GENERAL GEORGE S. PATTON

Mention risk taking in business and names like Richard Branson and Steve Jobs come to mind—legendary figures who've made big headlines and captured imaginations. Known for their vision and chutzpah, leaders like Branson and Jobs are risk taking personified—or so it would seem.

In reality, this type of risk taking is a minuscule fraction of all risk taking. Most risks are smaller and more common. They entail tackling the types of challenges or fears that people face every day: having a tough conversation to drive a project forward, conducting a difficult meeting to get to the bottom of an issue, or writing a business plan to start something new.

Even the big risks you see talked about in the popular business press aren't really that big. They're the final manifestation of a lot of previous smaller risks that you never hear about. The big risk that looks so daring is often nothing more than the final half-mile in a marathon of measured decisions. For example, Steve Jobs took many risks to bring the iPod, iPhone, and iPad to market, one of which was the years he spent developing and failing with the Newton. Successful risk takers usually take less visible risks, fail, and learn a lot before really hitting it big.

Bill Maris, a managing partner at Google Ventures (Google's venture capital arm), goes so far as to characterize his approach to risk taking as *not risking*. "To the outside world it might look like we're placing bets and crossing our fingers. That's not the case—when we make an investment, part of our job is to systematically identify and ameliorate the risks. By the time we take a 'risk' on a company, we've looked at so many angles that it doesn't actually feel like risk. It just feels like a really smart bet."

That's what smart risk taking is: going through a process of planning, experimenting, learning, and communicating so that you can make bets that are financially, emotionally, and logically smart *for you*.

De*risking* Risk Taking

Adopting the liberating mindsets of the power perception is the foundation for getting out of the comfort zone. But staying in the smart-risk zone is about more than mindsets; the next step is taking smart action.

At the core of smart risk taking is something that I call derisking, or removing as much uncertainty as you can at every stage of a risk. Removing uncertainty lowers fear and increases effectiveness and the likelihood of success. Derisking is what makes risk taking *smart*.

Derisking entails thoughtful reflection and preparation *before* taking the risk, combined with intentional learning and communication *during* and *after* taking it. Through years of consulting and coaching, I've found that smart risk takers consistently do five things well to derisk whatever they're up to. I call these the liberating actions of smart risk taking. Summarized here, these are the topics that I'll cover in the remainder of the book.

Find something worth fighting for. What do you care enough about to risk your time, energy, and possibly money to try to make happen? Finding something worth fighting for (I call it a SWFF) is the process of identifying and clarifying why risk taking is important to you in the first place. Smart risk takers understand that their emotional commitment to whatever they want to see happen is more than half the battle of getting it. You need something to motivate you when the effort becomes uncomfortable, as it inevitably will. Your SWFF has to be meaningful and inspiring.

See the future now. While SWFFs are inspiring, they tend to be too imprecise to drive focused action. Seeing the future now is the process of clarifying what exactly the big ideas mean in terms of real objectives, plans, and intended results. Where are you going? What's it going to look like when you get there? Which parts will be easy? Which will be tough? What are the critical things you can do now to increase your chances of success? Having a dialogue with team members, clients, partners, suppliers, and others is critical to being able to see the future now.

Act fast, learn fast. When you have an idea you're excited about, there's a tendency to want to jump in quickly with both feet, using a lot of resources up front. The moving quickly part is a good idea. However, using up too many resources right away isn't. It's a smarter idea to test pieces of your hypothesis rapidly so that you can learn what will and won't work before you put too much on the line. Inherent in testing ideas rapidly is seeing failure as a necessary step in the process, not an unfortunate result of it. Fast failures, designed to drive intentional learning, are part of the foundation for smart risk taking.

Communicate powerfully. Poor communication, while problematic in any situation, is even more detrimental in risk-taking scenarios, where things are changing quickly and small misunderstandings can have a magnified impact. Smart risk takers assume that communication is going to break down (because it always does) and plan accordingly. They get their thinking on the table early and often, probe to understand others' thinking, and don't shy away from the tough conversations.

Create a smart-risk culture. Risk taking, especially in an organizational context, is rarely an individual endeavor. Members of a team or a larger group need to share the same mindsets and values about expected behavior. For example, people need to know if it's OK to fail, and if so, what a smart failure looks like. Smart risk takers are aware that their behavior speaks louder than words and are vigilant about role modeling the right behavior.

While presented linearly, the five components of smart risk taking have a more dynamic relationship in execution. Finding something worth fighting for, seeing the future now, and acting fast and learning fast tend to inform and influence one another. For example, it might be through acting fast and learning fast that you see something critical about the future that you hadn't seen before. And as a result, you find something that's worth fighting for. These first three elements must be supported by powerful communication in order to survive.

Finally, a smart-risk culture is both an *output from* and *an input to* smart risk taking. Elements of a smart-risk culture must be alive in order to support initial attempts at risk taking. Then, subsequent risk taking strengthens this culture.

All five components of smart risk taking have an element of communication in them, whether directly or indirectly. At every stage of any risk, improving the way in which you discuss thoughts, plans, and actions is the single most effective way to derisk the risk, that is, to make it smart. Spreadsheets and models are important, but thinking and talking together are the most powerful risk-management tools any person or organization has.

As I'm sure is obvious by now, this book is not about broad corporate risk management, a topic that is well addressed elsewhere. Rather, it's about you, an individual, who may be running a team or organization and who needs to drive growth under uncertain circumstances and wants to make sure you're doing everything you can to succeed. Every solution included is something that I've road-tested with a variety of clients and something that you can put to use right away.

Learning How to Take Smart Risks

Because risk taking is difficult to understand as a set of abstract concepts, most of what follows are concrete stories demonstrating one or more smart-risk topics. Each story is focused on getting at the "DNA" of risk taking, that is, the thinking, decisions, and actions behind the scenes for the individuals, teams, and organizations that are trying to make something new happen. The majority of the stories are business-related, but the lessons are applicable to any individual or organization, large or small.

Throughout, I consider a risk taker to be someone who exhibits smart-risk-taking behaviors, regardless of whether or not she considers herself to have a "risk-taking" personality. Like Bill Maris, whom I mentioned earlier in this chapter, some of the best risk takers don't see themselves that way.

Furthermore, when risk taking is seen as a personality trait, it puts people into boxes—it implies that some people have the ability to take risks and others don't, which I don't believe is true. Everyone can push out of her comfort zone. Each person's smart-risk zone will be different; but everyone has one. That's why the x axis on the power perception diagram in Chapter 2 is perceived risk, not just risk. If you're pushing outside your comfort zone, you're taking a risk, no matter what your starting point. And if you're using the five components covered in this book, you're taking a smart risk.

IDEAS AND TOOLS FOR ACTION

Is Your Risk Taking Smart?

Following is a 15-question self-assessment (designed with a work setting in mind) to clarify specific places where your current behavior is helping or hindering smart risk taking.

Instructions

1. Think of a specific challenging project that you're working on. It should be something that has risk involved in the execution.
2. Check the box that best represents your level of agreement with each statement.
3. Go with your first "gut" reaction; it's usually the most indicative of your true thoughts and feelings.

With Regard to What You're Trying to Accomplish on a Specific Project or Initiative:	Strongly Agree	Agree	Disagree	Strongly Disagree
1. I'm taking time to reflect on where I want to go with the project.				
2. I feel a sense of urgency and importance to succeed with the project.				
3. I feel inspired and motivated by the project.				
4. I'm spending time outside of my office to get a sense of future trends or forces at play.				
5. I have a clear, documented description of the end goals I'm trying to reach.				
6. I have a good understanding of the pitfalls I may encounter in pursuit of these goals.				
7. I'm giving myself room to experiment and make mistakes.				
8. I'm generating "small wins" every week.				
9. I'm assessing actions taken in order to find critical learning opportunities.				
10. I have good communication structures in place (for example, productive and useful meetings, updates, and so on) to keep key players aligned.				
11. I'm up-front and honest about tough issues when I see them.				
12. I probe others' thinking to ensure that the tough issues they see are also on the table.				

With Regard to What You're Trying to Accomplish on a Specific Project or Initiative:	Strongly Agree	Agree	Disagree	Strongly Disagree
13. I support smart failures when they happen.				
14. I role model what I feel is smart-risk-taking behavior.				
15. I acknowledge and reward other people's risk-taking efforts.				

To Score Your Assessment

1. Assign points to each answer:
   ▶ Strongly agree = 4 points
   ▶ Agree = 3 points
   ▶ Disagree = 1 point
   ▶ Strongly disagree = 0 points
2. Tally subscale scores.

Find something worth fighting for:	Questions 1–3:	_____ out of 12
See the future now:	Questions 4–6:	_____ out of 12
Act fast, learn fast:	Questions 7–9:	_____ out of 12
Communicate powerfully:	Questions 10–12:	_____ out of 12
Create a smart-risk culture:	Questions 13–15:	_____ out of 12

3. Add subscale scores to get your final score.

   _____ out of 60

   Scoring Key

51–60	You're doing an *excellent* job of taking smart risks.
41–50	You're doing a *good* job of taking smart risks.
31–40	You're doing a *fair* job of taking smart risks.
21–30	You're doing a *poor* job of taking smart risks.
0–20	You're doing a *very poor* job of taking smart risks.

4. To get better at taking smart risks:
   a. Note your lowest single item scores. These are your areas for improvement.
   b. Pick one or two areas to work on initially.
   c. Use the content in the corresponding section of the book to find ways to improve and make progress.

Chapter 3 Summary

▶ Most risk taking is not the splashy stuff we see on the front pages of the popular business press. It's the smaller, more methodical risks of planning and experimenting over time.

▶ Derisking, or removing as much uncertainty as you can at every stage of a risk, is at the core of smart risk taking. Smart risk takers consistently do five things well to derisk whatever they're up to:

1. Find something worth fighting for (SWFF).
2. See the future now.
3. Act fast, learn fast.
4. Communicate powerfully.
5. Create a smart-risk culture.

▶ The five components of smart risk taking are nonlinear, informing and influencing one another continuously.

▶ Risk taking is not a personality trait, but rather an observable set of behaviors.

PART TWO

FIND SOMETHING WORTH FIGHTING FOR

CHAPTER FOUR

What Are You Willing to Fight For?

*Don't ask what the world needs. Ask what makes
you come alive, and go do that. Because what the
world needs is people who have come alive.*

—HOWARD THURMAN, American author,
educator, and activist

The American burying beetle is nature's most efficient recy-
cler. A 1½-inch nocturnal carrion insect, it depends on small
decaying animals such as birds and rodents as food sources
and nests for its eggs. In under an hour, a pair of burying
beetles can locate by scent a dead bird ten times their size,
defeather and embalm it with sticky saliva, dig a burial hole
for it, and lower it into the ground, using their legs as a con-
veyer belt. This becomes the home for their young to hatch
and feed before emerging as adults two months later.

Ecologically, the beetle's process does two critical things: it
returns important nutrients to the soil, and it keeps fly and ant
populations from reaching epidemic proportions. Scientists
call the burying beetle an "indicator species," one that serves
as an early warning signal for environmental problems.

At the turn of the twentieth century, the American burying beetle was found in more than thirty states in the eastern half of the United States. Now, because of habitat fragmentation and human food chain alteration, it's found in only six states and is on the endangered species list.

I'm not particularly interested in insects, but as my friend Molly shared this story over dinner one night, I couldn't help but be drawn in. Her infectious enthusiasm turned insects into truly compelling dinner conversation. Molly's genuine passion for and deep personal connection with these beetles reminded me that when someone has real energy behind the topic, anything can be interesting.

"Bugs are the underdogs of the ecological world," Molly explained. "They're everywhere, and they do so much good, yet so few of us realize it. Mostly we just want to step on them. Someone has to stand up for the bugs." Beaming proudly as she recalled her bugs' accomplishments over two college summers on Nantucket Island, you would've thought she was talking about her children if you'd missed the beginning of the conversation.

Looking back, Molly recalls this work as one of the most important developmental experiences of her life.

"My beetle work provided a life-changing context within which I grew personally and professionally," she reflected. "Finding and recruiting volunteers, running the project team, collecting and analyzing data, as well as some other disgusting tasks, were tough challenges, but ultimately they were very rewarding. If you'd asked me before if I thought I could do what I did, I would have said no. I'd never done anything like that before. I felt like I was out of my comfort zone every single day. The enduring lesson I took away from my work with beetles was that I have the ability to rise to the occasion if something is important enough to me."

Molly's story illustrates an age-old truism: when you find something worth fighting for (or SWFF), it can change you (even if it's bugs). You get a playground and laboratory for experimentation. You have opportunities to stretch, grow, and gain confidence. In short, you find a worthwhile reason to risk.

At the same time, having a SWFF is also a reminder that the converse is true. When you don't have something worth fighting for, you stagnate because you have little reason to risk, stretch, and grow.

The Meaning in Life

Whether you're trying to build your organization, excel in a personal hobby, or do anything else that's important to you, SWFFs are key because they provide boundaries within which you can play, extend yourself, and truly "go for it." In a world of infinite places where you could put your energy, a SWFF is your declaration that *this* is the place where you're going to put it. When you choose and commit to a SWFF, it reorients your thinking about what risks you're willing to take to make something happen. You can't take risks in every aspect of your life, so where are the critical few?

The power of Molly's SWFF came alive because of her deep personal relationship to it. When you're plugged in and engaged in something that's important to you, you feel that what you say and do not only makes sense, but also makes a difference. Without this commitment, you're like a ship without a compass, adrift and unable to figure out where to go and what to do next. SWFFs aren't just things it might be nice to have. They're fundamental to your sense of meaning.

Meaning can be looked at in two ways.[1] One way is the philosophical "meaning *of* life." Plato believed that the meaning of life was attained through knowledge. Antisthenes said that meaning came from a life of virtue. Kant thought it was based on a sense of duty. Nietzsche, a nihilist, believed that there was no inherent meaning of life. These theories are intellectually stimulating. You could sit around and talk about them for hours. But they're too broad and abstract to be useful on a daily basis. They don't help you figure out where to put your feet when you roll out of bed each morning.

The second, more modest and arguably more useful way to look at meaning considers the meaning *in* life. It refers to where individuals find *personal* purpose and significance. In my work as a coach and consultant, I've found that people tend to find meaning in life when (1) they're pursuing an important, challenging goal, (2) they feel effective and competent in that pursuit, and (3) they're making a positive impact or contribution.

Like a three-legged stool, all three of these aspects of meaning are necessary for us to find meaning in something over the long term. Alone, any one of them can be rewarding. But over time, all three together are needed for a truly fulfilling life. When you don't have all three, you experience a gap in meaning.

You feel a gap, for example, if you're pursuing a challenging and important goal, but you aren't getting more effective or competent in the pursuit. You feel a gap if you're great at what you do, but it's not challenging or important. And you also feel a gap if you're doing something that's important and challenging, but it's not making a positive impact on others. Only all three together give you something worth fighting for.

So how do you find what holds personal meaning for you?

How to Find a Meaningful SWFF

In my experience, people come across the things they're willing to fight for in one of three ways: destiny, delivery, or discovery. The first two are SWFFs that get dropped in your lap. Either (1) you know what you want to do from an extremely young age (destiny) or (2) you're put in a life-altering tough spot and have to fight your way out (delivery). Most of us don't find our SWFFs in these ways. Rather, we have to roll up our sleeves and go out to find them (discovery).

Destined SWFFs

People who find SWFFs through destiny somehow know what they're meant to do from very early in life. Child prodigies fall into this group. Mozart could play an entire Wagenseil scherzo by age four. At five, he was composing his own works. And by six, he was performing for the eighteenth-century courts of Europe. Pablo Picasso learned to paint at age seven. By eight, he had painted *Le Picador*, and by thirteen, he had far surpassed his father, an accomplished artist in his own right. Ice hockey star Wayne Gretzky learned to shoot a puck at age two. By six, he was one of the best players in a league of ten-year-olds. By thirteen, he had scored more than one thousand goals in the Canadian minor hockey leagues.

Famous people with destined SWFFs always have high entertainment value; we love to hear their inspiring stories. However, destined SWFFs are extremely rare. That level of early clarity is inaccessible to the vast majority of us. Most of us have to search around much longer before we find the SWFFs that are meant for us.

Delivered SWFFs

Delivered SWFFs initially show up as a battle rather than a passion. They're usually something we were neither looking for nor eager to receive. But once we have them, they shape our lives forever. Health issues and social causes are common precipitating forces. While it is typically not the sole driver of meaning in someone's life, a delivered SWFF can become a large part of it, providing a newfound mission and sense of purpose.

Nancy Brinker is an example of someone who had a delivered SWFF. Her sister, Susan G. Komen, died of breast cancer in 1982. Susan's last wish was that Nancy work to transform the way the world talks about and treats the disease, which was being ignored at the time. Brinker's promise to her sister was that she would "change this [even] if it takes the rest of my life."

Brinker founded the Susan G. Komen for the Cure organization in 1982 to raise money for breast cancer education. But every charity she approached said that it wasn't interested in supporting her. That's when she came up with the idea for the Race for the Cure charity events that have since raised billions of dollars for breast cancer research and support.

Under Brinker's leadership, the organization has been a driving force in more than doubling the number of women receiving early breast cancer detection exams, turning millions of breast cancer patients into cancer survivors. In 2008 *Time* magazine named Nancy Brinker one of the 100 Most Influential People in the World.

Similarly, Lois Gibbs had a delivered SWFF in 1978 when this then 27-year-old homemaker learned that her neighborhood in Niagara Falls, New York, was built on 20,000 tons of toxic waste. With only a high school education and no previous political experience, but determined to do something about it, she organized the Love Canal Homeowners Association. For two years, while being publicly vilified as a "hysterical housewife," she fought the Occidental Petroleum Corporation as well as state, local, and federal governments that claimed that the toxic waste wasn't to blame for surges in birth defects and other disabling ailments in her community. Finally in 1980, due largely to Gibbs's tireless work, President Jimmy Carter issued an emergency declaration and moved all 900 families into new homes away from the toxins. Gibbs's efforts ultimately paved the way for the Superfund Program, which permanently changed the way toxic waste is viewed and handled in the United States. In 1981, Gibbs moved to Washington, D.C., to found the Center for Health, Environment, & Justice, a powerful environmental organization that she still runs to this day.

One of the most moving accounts of a delivered SWFF is that of Viennese psychiatrist Viktor Frankl, who was interned in Nazi concentration camps during World War II. Frankl recounts his moving story in his popular book *Man's Search for Meaning*, first published in 1946.[2] For almost three years he endured starvation, frostbite, serious illness, and mental torture. Every day for 945 days straight was a living hell. Yet he survived when millions of others did not. How did he do it?

After a few months in the camps, Frankl realized that his will to live would never be enough to keep him alive. He knew that the horrible situation would break his spirit too quickly. He needed to find a deeper motivation to survive, a bigger SWFF beyond himself that would make his struggles worthwhile and give him a compelling reason to hang on. Each day he saw that those who couldn't find a bigger SWFF quickly lost their fight to live.

Frankl's SWFF was born from his training as a psychiatrist. He realized that he might be the only person with his training to be witnessing such heinous acts. He felt that he had a duty to learn from the experience—not for himself, but for humanity. He chose to use the horrors he saw to understand the human condition of both victims and persecutors. That choice revealed not only appalling cruelty, but also the height of human resilience. Exposure to the repulsive worst that humanity is capable of also provided him with a profound appreciation for the strength that people can summon when they have something that is worth fighting for.

Frankl found his insights so powerful that after the war, he created his own brand of psychotherapy, which he called logotherapy (that is, meaning therapy). Logotherapy helped patients make sense of their lives—where they'd been, where they were, and where they wanted to go. As patients planned for the future, he would ask them a simple yet provocative question, "Why don't you kill yourself?" He wasn't asking the question to be cruel. He was asking it because he wanted his patients to connect with what they were willing to fight for. Better than anyone else, he knew that their survival lay in their answer to that blunt question. What was keeping them alive? What inspired them? What made them happy? Ultimately Frankl's SWFF became helping other people find theirs.

Discovered SWFFs

Viktor Frankl's insight and famous question point to the third and most common way to find SWFFs—by discovery. When destiny and delivery don't bring the inspiration you need, you must go out and find it yourself. Many people take an academic or apprentice route. Some follow in a parent's footsteps. Others turn a hobby into a business. And still others make it up as they go along, finding opportunities where they can. It doesn't matter who you are or where you've been; everyone has the opportunity to find meaningful

SWFFs. All that's required is openness to exploration and acceptance of the idea that it's never too late to find what lights you up.

If you ever find yourself thinking that you've missed an opportunity or that life has passed you by (and you're now too old to do anything about it), think again. You can discover your SWFFs at any time in life.

Consider Colonel Harlan Sanders, who didn't start Kentucky Fried Chicken until he was in his sixties. For 20 years before that, he had fed his budding love for cooking by making chicken for travelers who stopped by the service station and motel restaurant where he worked. By that time, he'd already held jobs as a steamboat pilot, insurance salesman, fireman, and farmer.

Similarly, Laura Ingalls Wilder didn't write her first and most famous book, *Little House on the Prairie*, until she was also in her sixties. It wasn't until she was in her forties that she began writing when she took a job as a columnist at the *Missouri Ruralist* newspaper.

There's always a SWFF that can inspire you if you're willing to put in the time and energy to look for it. The suggestions and exercises at the end of this chapter can help you in that process, whether you're looking to find a new SWFF or to grow an existing one.

No matter how you come across your SWFF, once you've found one, SWFFs all require a proactive choice to engage. This final step is always the toughest. Contrary to popular belief, nobody has it easy when it comes to finding a SWFF.

A destined SWFF can feel like a weight that robs you of your freedom to explore. A delivered SWFF can feel like something you never asked for and would desperately like to undo. A discovered SWFF can feel like too much work to identify as you try out and discard many possibilities.

Despite the work involved in any SWFF, the only mistake you can make is not choosing to engage in something. If you have a delivered SWFF and you don't want to battle it, that's fine. Go out and discover a different one. If you don't want to follow a destined SWFF or pursue a discovered SWFF from your past, that's fine, too. It's only through continuously choosing to engage in something inspiring that we find meaning. This commitment is a defining moment in any worthwhile fight and the fundamental risk that we all need to take.

IDEAS AND TOOLS FOR ACTION

Get Clear on What You Value

We all have a set of values that govern our lives. When they're present, they make us feel engaged and alive. These might be things like adventure, creativity, accomplishment, or excellence. Unfortunately, as life gets more hectic, you can lose sight of these touchstones as the minutiae of daily life take over. Before you know it, experiences that really light you up can become distant memories.

Because values are leading indicators of SWFFs, it's important that you take the time to identify and reconnect to them.

One of the best ways to get back in touch with your values is through stories about times when you felt really alive. These experiences carry the DNA of what you value most. They can be personal, work-related, school-related, or whatever, as long as they describe times when you felt really lit up.

Here's an exercise for getting clear on what you value:

1. Begin by finishing this statement:
   a. A time in my life when I felt really alive was _____.
      (Try to answer this at least three to five times.)
   b. For each, give some detail:
      i. What were you doing?
      ii. Who were you with?
      iii. What did you achieve and/or learn?
2. Look at your answers and identify values that you feel are present. The following is a list of values to spark your thinking. Circle your top 5 to 10. (Feel free to add any additional ones that you don't see here.) When you're

done, prioritize them. This will help you get clear on what's most important to you.

Accountability	Flexibility	Nature
Achievement	Forgiveness	Openness
Adventure	Freedom	Order
Affection	Friendship	Partnership
Authenticity	Fun	Passion
Balance	Generosity	Patience
Beauty	Genuineness	Perseverance
Challenge	Growth	Play
Collaboration	Happiness	Pleasure
Compassion	Health	Prestige
Competition	Honesty	Quality
Confidence	Honor	Reflection
Contribution	Humility	Respect
Cooperation	Humor	Responsibility
Courage	Independence	Serenity
Creativity	Influence	Service
Curiosity	Inspiration	Spirituality
Decisiveness	Integrity	Status
Development	Involvement	Success
Discipline	Joy	Teamwork
Efficiency	Kindness	Tolerance
Empathy	Knowledge	Tradition
Excellence	Leadership	Trust
Enthusiasm	Loyalty	Variety
Family	Moderation	Wisdom

3. Which of these values have you let slip out of your life?

As you look at your values list, you'll probably see some that are still present in your life. You'll also see others that you've lost touch with. An example might be that you love feeling a sense of challenge, but that you haven't felt it in a while. Put a check mark next to the ones you've let slip out of your life that you'd like to get back.

Go Inspire Yourself

The Latin root of the word *inspiration* means "to breathe life into." That's exactly what inspiring people, places, and situations do to you. They wake you up and give you a different perspective. When you feel inspired, you're more likely to think creatively and connect with a SWFF.

Inspiration can come from anywhere—reading a great book, listening to a motivating speaker, standing inside a beautiful building, looking at an intriguing piece of art, singing, dancing, or playing sports. The list is long. While you might not be able to control or predict just what will inspire you, you can certainly put yourself in situations where inspiration is more likely to happen.

The following are inspirational experiences I've collected from clients through the years, along with an explanation for why they found them so inspiring:

> ► There's something magical to me about the *back bowls at Vail*. I made the decision that I was going to propose to my wife while skiing there. Nine years later, while I was there, on the same slope, I think, I also made the decision to open my art gallery. I find clarity on the ski slopes that I can't find anywhere else.
> ► I like to sit in one of the restaurants on the second floor of *Grand Central Terminal in New York City* and just take in the people and the architecture. I feel like I'm connecting to a bygone era of businesspeople who had more guts and chutzpah than we do today. I feel a renewed sense of vigor when I go back to the office.
> ► I love *poetry readings* because there are no rules. It's just pure self-expression. This is the opposite of my everyday life as an IT executive at a bank. In a way, I think it makes me a better executive because it reminds me that there's a creative aspect to the work I do. I've never stopped to think about it, but I'd bet that some of the biggest, riskiest changes I've made in my department came on the heels of attending poetry readings.
> ► As a kid, I used to go to the *Kettle Moraine Forest* north of Milwaukee to hike and camp. I can still see my dad pointing out insects, plants, and trees and telling me about them. These are really fond memories. I try to return every few years and take my kids now. We have a great time, and

it clears my head. It reminds me of the importance of the simple things in life—a SWFF in and of itself.

▶ We have quarterly *Future Focus Meetings* with our management team. They're well-structured, well-run meetings. But they do more than help us plan for the future. They give me an opportunity to get reinvigorated by the members of our team—hearing their thinking for the road ahead. I always leave those meetings with more spring in my step and fire in my belly. It's a great reminder of why I love this company.

Solict Insights From Others

Other people see things about us that we often don't see. These can be great insights that can help us find our SWFFs. Others might see things that we're really good at, but that we take for granted. They may see that we spend too much time on things we hate to do or that we've totally lost touch with certain things we love to do. We miss these insights because we're too caught up in the everyday demands of our lives. Others who know us have the advantage of being able to see us from 10,000 feet up, without getting stuck in the minutiae we're swimming in. They can see a forest where we see only trees, or even just leaves and bark.

Most of the time people don't share these insights with us. They watch us for days, weeks, months, and even years without saying anything. We do the same thing; we watch them and say nothing. Why? Because unsolicited advice is generally not welcome. Sure, in the right situations, with the right people, and with the right up-front framing, advice giving can work, but more often than not, it's just perceived as irritating.

That's why you've got to get good at soliciting feedback.

The more you solicit insights and advice from others, the less work you have to do racking your brain to figure things out, the more perspective you get, the more angles you can see, and the better-informed decisions you make. All of these things are critical to discovering your SWFFs.

Most of us tend not to ask people for advice because we don't want them to point out our flaws. Usually our shortcomings are so painfully clear in our own minds that we'd understandably rather not have them brought to life in words. But other people actually see more than just your flaws. They also see nuances in your strengths that you've probably never considered. They make connections that you don't make. They see opportunities that you've overlooked. And when they do point out a flaw, it's rarely as bad as you think it is. Discussing your shortcomings has a way of decreasing their power over you. You realize that everyone has them and they're not something to get so worked up over.

How to Ask Others for Their Insights About You

Use these questions to interview others. Feel free to add different questions if you'd like, but don't ask more than 10 total:

1. What do you think I'm really good at?
2. What do you think I'm bad at?
3. Have I had a positive impact on you? If so, how and where? If not, why not?
4. Is there anything I used to love to do that you feel I've lost touch with?
5. Knowing me, where do you think I should focus my energy over the next 5 to 10 years?

Note: The most important thing in doing your interviews is setting them up effectively. Here are four tips on how to do that:

- ▶ *Pick people who you think are insightful.* This seems obvious, but it's worth stating. Someone who is not reflective and doesn't know himself very well will have a tough time giving you astute observations about you.
- ▶ *Tell them clearly why you're interviewing them.* If you don't do this, it will seem weird for you to ask these questions, and you probably won't get the type of answers you're looking for. Say something like, "I'm exploring opportunities for _____ (a new career, how to give

back, new hobbies, or something similar), and I'd love some of your insights about me. I've got five questions I'd like to ask you. Do you have 15 minutes to chat?"

▶ *Ask them to shoot straight.* People are conditioned to sugarcoat things to get by in society. But if these interviews are to be helpful to you, you don't want disengaged and vague "nice" comments. You want real feedback (both complimentary and critical). So ask directly for it.

▶ *Probe their answers to get specifics.* If someone says she's always admired or hated a certain quality in you, ask for specifics. In what situations? At what times? Can you give me examples? Again, vague, general feedback is much less useful to you.

Chapter 4 Summary

▶ SWFFs change us. They provide us with a playground and laboratory for experimentation. They give us a reason to risk, providing opportunities to stretch, grow, and gain confidence.

▶ You find lasting SWFFs that give your life meaning when (1) you're pursuing a challenging goal that's important to you, (2) you feel effective and competent in that pursuit, and (3) you're making a positive impact or contribution. All three are needed.

▶ We can find our SWFFs in three ways: destiny, delivery, or discovery.

▶ Getting clear on what you value is a good way to discover a SWFF because, by definition, we'll fight for the things we value.

▶ Another strategy for discovering a SWFF is to put yourself in inspiring situations that breathe life into you and get your creative energy flowing.

▶ A third strategy for discovering a SWFF is to interview other people about you. Others see things about you that you don't see.

Finding the Fight in Your Organization

If you want to build a ship, don't drum up people to collect wood and don't assign them tasks and work, but rather teach them to long for the endless immensity of the sea.

—ANTOINE DE SAINT-EXUPÉRY, French writer and aviator

When I walk into an organization, I can usually tell within a few minutes whether it's got something worth fighting for. I can see it in the way a receptionist greets me and in the conversations I hear between employees. Do they sound like they're up to something? Is there engagement in their voices? I can even see it in the physical environment. Does the place draw me in, give me a shot of energy, and give me the sense that something special is going on? Unfortunately, the conclusion I come to in many organizations is a resounding "no" on all counts.

Having something that's worth fighting for is critical for creating smart and sustained risk taking in an organization. Without a SWFF, it's just too easy for people to look at challenges as too difficult to overcome and not worth the risk to pursue or address.

What Makes for a Good SWFF in an Organization?

SWFFs come in all shapes and sizes, but in general, they share four characteristics.

First and most important, a good SWFF *stirs emotion*. It connects to basic human desires to win, be engaged, and feel alive, like what we're doing has meaning. It's not enough for the senior leaders of an organization to be excited about the prospects of successfully pursuing some business if those below merely feel like cogs carrying out someone else's plan. Before too long, these people won't feel any emotional connection to the work and won't go above and beyond to make things happen. It's the job of senior leaders to ensure that they're connecting the behavior in the organization to emotions that we all want to feel—excitement, engagement, pride, and passion.

Two strong emotional foundations tend to generate SWFFs: the desire to either build something or beat something. Usually it's a little of both. Think of your work right now. Do you have either or both of these emotions? Do those around you share it? If not, you're probably missing a SWFF.

Second, a good SWFF *is story-based*. Only stories convey emotion and get people excited; statistics and data don't. When you and those around the organization talk about a SWFF, tell it as a story. Share the background. Why is this topic important to you? How did you come to your conclusions? What emotion did it bring up in you? How did you get to where you are? Where are you going, and why?

Good storytelling takes a tough and banal set of tasks and strings a meaningful narrative thread through them. French writer Antoine de Saint-Exupéry captured this idea well in the opening quote of this chapter: "If you want to build a ship, don't drum up people to collect wood and don't assign them tasks and work, but rather teach them to long for the endless immensity of the sea." Only stories can create that longing.

Third, a good SWFF *is simple*. It's something that a first grader can understand. A first grader may not understand all the implications of it, like how you're going to pursue it or why it's so important, but she'll be able to understand what you are saying. She can understand the idea of being down but not out, for example. She can understand the idea of wanting to win in an important competition. She can understand the desire to change people's lives for the better.

Getting a SWFF down to the level of a first grader is important because in reality, we're all like first graders. While we may have more ability to understand complex issues than they do, we don't have the time. We're bombarded with information all day every day—all of it vying for our attention. Scanning our environments to figure out where to put our attention, we tend to gravitate toward ideas and people that we can connect to easily and that make immediate sense.

If you had to put it down in words, a good SWFF is usually no more than a few sentences. As a rule of thumb, it shouldn't take lengthy documents or complex diagrams to explain a SWFF. The more you need to engage someone's analytical mind to convey a SWFF, the weaker it gets. In fact, I've noticed an inverse relationship between the amount of documentation used to explain an idea and the ability to get people excited about it. Of course, when you get to the strategic planning stages, you will need analytical firepower. But you don't need so much at the SWFF stage.

Finally, a good SWFF *inspires action*. It provides a context for the bumps on the road ahead. Even if things aren't easy, there's still a compelling reason to keep moving forward. This is how you know you've got a good SWFF: people are visibly fighting for it. They're taking the time and energy to do the things I talk about in the rest of this book. They're making decisions in the face of uncertainly, raising tough questions, seeing pitfalls and heading them off, making themselves a little uncomfortable, failing, and learning.

Does your organization have meaningful SWFFs? If not, you need to work on getting some, or on taking the ones you have and making them clearer, stronger, and more compelling.[1]

The three stories that follow give you an idea of what a SWFF can look like. Each is from a different business, of a different size, with different issues. But they all have the four characteristics just discussed, which created a fighting spirit.

A Struggling Division Fights Back to a Top Position

Menasha Packaging is the largest division of the 160-year-old, $1 billion Menasha Corporation. It develops packaging and retail display solutions for food and healthcare companies. Once known as a middle-of-the-pack player in a zero-growth market, it has transformed itself into an innovative powerhouse over the last seven years, largely because it almost ceased to exist as part of Menasha Corporation.

In 2005, unable to compete with the larger players in its market, Menasha Packaging was put up for sale. It was an uncomfortable spot for a proud family company. What made the situation worse was the fact that few buyers were interested. Menasha's products were perceived as commodities. At one point the company found a buyer, but then the deal fell through at the last minute. No other attractive suitors were on the horizon.

Mike Waite, president of Menasha Packaging, wasn't quite sure where to go next. He sat down with his chairman, and they came to the conclusion that no one was coming to rescue them. They had to make this thing work. Waite gathered his leadership team to consider options for the road ahead.

"That first meeting was painful," Waite recalls. "Everyone felt like they'd gotten hit in the gut. Not only had we failed to sell the company, but now we had to figure out how to grow it."

After some requisite frank conversations, a fighting spirit slowly started to emerge within the leadership team. Something that the scuttled sale's due diligence helped the team realize was just how strong the company's customer relationships were. Surprisingly, the company that had almost bought it hadn't valued this asset very highly. It made Menasha realize that the potential acquirer would have destroyed the relationships. It dawned on the leadership team that Menasha didn't have to keep playing in the commodity packaging market. It was well positioned to build a big business in delivering custom solutions. It could be a growth business, and something worth fighting for—if the leaders could get the rest of the organization behind it. However, that was a big if.

The stark fact was that the leaders had just tried to sell a 160-year-old division of a family company where employees felt like part of the family. Many of them had worked there for 20 to 40 years. Employee sentiment was not positive. It could be summed up as, "We're part of a 160-year-old firm based on strong family values. We hit a rough patch for a little while, and you try to break up the family? How could you do that to us and to the company?" Employees had lost their trust in Waite and the management team. Any chance of rebuilding the company had to start with rebuilding trust with each and every employee.

Trust became the heart of the new SWFF—the cornerstone that would make or break the company. As Waite and his leadership team developed and rolled out the new strategy, employees were engaged at every step of the way—from initial ideation to detailed execution.

"We went out to every plant and met with every shift to discuss the new strategy, engaging 1,800 people one small group at a time," Waite shared. "It accomplished a few critical things. It allowed them to provide input. It helped them understand our thinking and why we had made certain decisions. But, most important, it reengaged their hearts, minds, and fighting spirits."

That last point was pivotal. Waite had always known that Menasha employees were a hard-working, dedicated bunch. But the near sale brought the depth of their dedication into clearer focus. These employees loved competition and wanted to fight for the company. They believed strongly in the family values that were at its foundation and shuddered at the thought of another company running the place. That employee spirit, in turn, gave Waite and his leadership team a shot in the arm. More than any product goals, they wanted to fight for the employees who were willing to fight for Menasha. It gave the leadership the courage to continue to focus the company and make tough decisions to grow it.

The results from the SWFF showed up quickly. Within 14 months, profits had doubled. Over the next several years, even during the recession, sales increased each year. What's more, the spirit throughout the organization was transformed. You could feel a level of excitement and engagement as you walked the floors. People were up to something important.

Seeing Weakness, a Bank Makes Critical Changes in Technology

SWFFs like Menasha's are drastic existential threats to a business. They're hard to deal with, but in many ways that makes them easier to rally around. Options are few. As mentioned in the previous chapter, Menasha's would be an example of a *delivered* SWFF. Often organizational SWFFs aren't that obvious. You have to do some digging to discover and clarify them.

Several years ago, I was part of a team that worked with a large global bank to help it transform the technology operations of a key division. One of our early findings was that, compared to other banks, this bank was putting a significantly smaller percentage of its budget into customer-focused innovation, and this was putting it in a bad competitive position.

We presented the requisite pretty charts and graphs to illustrate these points to the IT group. Our basic conclusion was, you're going to lose money and customers soon if you don't change course. We got a lot of head nods in agreement. Everyone thought it made a lot of sense. The general consensus walking out of the presentation that day was, *we should do something about this.*

Our consulting team felt good about the analysis, but at the same time, we knew that the IT group didn't have a SWFF yet. All it had were statistics, data, and a few key insights. These things alone wouldn't be compelling enough to get it up the mountain it needed to climb. The changes the bank needed to make were risky. It would have to start making tough decisions about how to fund the innovation, which would affect existing budgets and processes. Feathers were about to get ruffled.

The CIO saw this coming. "How do I get the people on my team to really understand that these changes have to happen, that these aren't a 'nice to have'? I know they all get it rationally, but when the budgets start shifting, these guys are going to dig in, resist the changes, and passive-aggressively sabotage the effort. I need to light a fire underneath them."

We helped kindle that fire at a joint IT/business offsite. Leaders from the business units joined the IT executives to have an open conversation about the good, the bad, and the ugly regarding IT's performance. Our hope was that we could facilitate conversations that would bring a SWFF in hard-hitting language to the surface.

Ninety minutes into the conversation, we found what we were looking for. After a lively exchange, one business executive said, "I'm embarrassed to tell clients about our technology. It's clearly inferior to our competitors' in some pretty fundamental ways." The room went silent for a few seconds (although it felt more like a few minutes). In this company, comments like that were rare. I wasn't sure what would happen. Would the observation get quickly swept under the rug? Would someone pipe up to soften the blow? Or would others jump on the bandwagon? Thankfully, a few more people piled on. I say thankfully because it was an authentic statement that needed to land with an impact.

An hourlong discussion ensued, the likes of which had never happened between these two groups before. They discussed specific places where the technology had fallen behind and what customers had said. It stung both IT and the business group to hear this. Both groups realized that they had been complicit in not raising the issues effectively over the previous few years. Their competitive natures stoked, by the end of the day the spirit in the room had changed considerably.

Acknowledging the errors of their ways, both groups wanted to right the ship together. They both wanted to identify the specific places where they could start winning again and beat the competition. Their goal was not just something that was logically worth pursuing. It was something that they all really wanted to fight for, and it formed the foundation for a successful 18-month change process.

Building an Investment Firm Whose Time Had Come

All SWFFs need to inspire and motivate. Sometimes that feels doubly important at start-ups, where everything can feel like it's working against you.

By most accounts, Jono Steinberg shouldn't have succeeded in transforming WisdomTree into an asset management company. While it's now the seventh-largest provider of exchange-traded funds (ETFs), with more than $15 billion in assets under management, eight years ago WisdomTree had little traction, money, or prospects of ever making it.

All it had was an idea worth fighting for.

The WisdomTree story starts in 1997, when, as the CEO of Individual Investor Group (INDI), Steinberg began constructing fundamentally weighted stock indexes based on dividends and earnings rather than on the more common market capitalization. At the time, INDI was a financial publisher. The plan was to sell these indexes as information products to asset management companies. It hadn't yet occurred to Steinberg that *he* could be the asset management company.

Two things happened to change his thinking.

First, after testing his indexes, he found that they could generate a better after-fee return than Vanguard's—a coveted measuring stick for retail investors. Second, even though ETFs were a superior investment vehicle for tax, transparency, fee, and liquidity reasons, very few asset management companies were marketing them at that time. And the ones that were marketing them weren't using indexes like his.

Steinberg quickly realized that he was sitting on a big idea that he was uniquely positioned to take advantage of. Rather than providing information, he could become the actual asset management company—a much bigger business opportunity. He knew his indexes were winners. The billion-dollar question was, could he actually build a company around them?

In 2001, Steinberg decided to sell off his publication business and give it a shot.

He began with several strikes against him that could have sunk his efforts at any point. He hadn't managed money in years, and he wasn't part of a large, trusted financial institution. And, most challenging, he had nowhere near enough capital to do what he was about to do.

To get a fighting chance, Steinberg whittled INDI down to three people. For two years, he pushed forward, building the company from his own bank account and a few outside supporters. The linchpin for success was finding heavy-hitter investors to back the business. Steinberg knew that raising capital would be tough, but he underestimated just how tough it would be. His biggest hurdle was that the theory seemed too simple and too good to be true. Few people were interested.

Furthermore, Steinberg wouldn't do preferred stock deals or create a separate entity for new shareholders. Both were requested by nearly every potential investor, and both would have made it easier to raise money. But INDI was a public company, and its shareholders owned the indexes. Steinberg was adamant that diluting their share or trying to cut them out of the deal was morally wrong.

By mid-2004, INDI's stock was worth 3 cents a share. The company was basically bankrupt. Steinberg's personal savings were gone as well.

"I was getting no encouragement from the market," Steinberg recalls. "Worse, there were naysayers everywhere. To say it was challenging is an understatement. But throughout, we never doubted the idea as a better way for people to invest—that was a constant."

Steinberg's breakthrough came in late 2004 when noted Wharton finance professor Jeremy Siegel validated the theories behind INDI's research. Soon RRE Ventures, a venture capital firm cofounded by James Robinson III, the former CEO of American Express, and Michael Steinhardt, a legendary hedge fund investor, agreed to invest working capital to keep Steinberg afloat based on the power of INDI's theories, now validated by research. In one day, based on the announcement of this investment, INDI went from a $1 million valuation to more than $120 million.

However, INDI wasn't out of the woods yet. It took another two grueling years before it got its first ETFs launched. While shareholders waited anxiously for progress, Steinberg scrambled to get operations in place to start marketing the funds and accepting client money. Most frustrating was the glacial pace of the SEC approval that it needed in order to list its funds.

In 2006, it launched its first 20 equity ETFs, the largest single-day launch on the NYSE. It also changed the company name to WisdomTree. At that point, other ETF companies had been educating the market, so investors were very receptive to the new products that WisdomTree offered. Money started flowing in.

Then, just when Steinberg thought he was at last on a roll, the recession of 2008 hit. After a few more precarious bumps, including experiencing the ETF complex's only quarter of net outflows, WisdomTree turned cash flow positive in the second quarter of 2010. In 2011, it finally turned profitable and listed on the Nasdaq Global Market. Success had been a long time coming—14 years after Steinberg had first conceived of the indexes and 9 years after he'd started to pursue them as an asset management company.

"It was a lot of hard work to make WisdomTree a reality, more than I could have ever imagined," Steinberg shared, reflecting back over the years. "Ultimately, I think our story is a testament to the power of deeply believing in something. It gave us the conviction to keep going when so many other signs told us to stop."

Is a SWFF the Same as a Mission, Vision, or Purpose?

As you can tell from these stories, SWFFs are powerful drivers of mindsets and behaviors. They're beacons that provide direction when things are tough. And people usually point to them as an essential ingredient in success.

I'm often asked if a SWFF is the same as a mission, vision, purpose, or any number of other direction-setting activities popular in organizations. The answer is maybe, but not necessarily.

In some organizations, a SWFF is the same as these things. For example, when your mission is alive and kicking in the organization—when people know it cold, live it, and are fighting for it—your mission is a SWFF. The same goes for a vision or a purpose.

However, if a group of employees in relative isolation has wordsmithed any of these things, hung them on a wall, and done little else, your vision, mission, or purpose most likely is *not* a SWFF. The ideas may be good, but they're not things that people will fight for. In the best cases, this is because people don't internalize missions and the like that are created this way. In the worst cases, it's because these documents aren't actually true. They're aspirational wish lists or something that was merely written to sound good.

IDEAS AND TOOLS FOR ACTION

Look Back from the Future

If you don't feel as though you and/or your organization has a SWFF, this exercise can help jump-start your thinking. You can do it alone or in a group.

Imagine it's 10 years from today. You're looking back over the last decade in business, and unfortunately, you have some regrets. Overall, it's been a good 10 years, but you do wish you had taken more chances in one or two important areas—and tried harder to make something happen.

1. Reflect on the following question: *looking back, given what you know about yourself, your team, and your organization, what do you think you might be regretting?* Try to be as

specific as possible. Write it in the past tense, as if you really are in the future looking back. (For example, "We didn't do this," or, "We failed to get this off the ground.")

2. What advice would your future self give your present-day self? Again, the more specific you can be, the better.

3. Rephrase the regret and advice as a SWFF.

To make it a little more concrete, here's an illustrative example of how Jono Steinberg in the story earlier in this chapter *might have* used this exercise in 2000 to imagine what his 2010 self could be seeing or telling him regarding his indexes.

The regret looking back from the future. As I look back over the last 10 years, I regret that we never did much with those indexes. We continued to try to sell them as information products, but with content becoming such a commodity, it never really took off. I wish we had taken a shot at trying to become an asset management company ourselves before the ETF market mushroomed.

The advice from his 2010 self to his 2000 self. Find a way to take those indexes to market as an asset management company yourself. You've done the research, you have a lot of conviction that it's a good idea, and no one else is doing it. As scary as the prospect seems, you're going to regret it if it turns out that you were onto a big idea and you never did anything about it.

Rephrased as a SWFF in 2000. I've been thinking about this idea for a few years now, and I am sure that I'm onto to a good idea. Let's take a shot at trying to get it off the ground.

Get Better at Storytelling

If you feel that you already have a SWFF, but you are struggling to engage and enroll others in it, try improving your storytelling skills.

Chatting with a seatmate on a plane recently, I came across a great example of how a story can convey a SWFF. After a brief conversation, I asked my seatmate what he did. His name was Justin Welsh, and he was the California sales manager for ZocDoc, a service that offers doctors' appointments instantly online. It had been a long week, I was tired, and I'm sure he saw my eyes start to glaze over a bit. He immediately relayed the story of how the company came to be.

The founder, Cyrus Massoumi, was on a flight back home to New York when his eardrum popped. Upon landing, not knowing any ear, nose, and throat doctors, he frantically started visiting websites and dialing doctors' offices. At one after another, he was put on hold and told that the first available appointment was a month or more away. It was days later before he found a doctor who would see him. ZocDoc was designed to cut out the headaches of finding and scheduling doctors' appointments.

As I listened to the story, I thought to myself, what a great service. These were all frustrations that I'd had before. In an instant, I understood the reason for the company and exactly what it could provide for me—on an emotional level.

Now, if Welsh had kept going with a dry description of how the service could provide a more timely experience for patients and more efficiency for the doctors' staff, I probably would have fallen asleep halfway through the first sentence. It would have been accurate, but it would have been really boring. He would have left me to do the hard work of figuring out why I really cared, and that was something I wasn't particularly motivated to do.

In all fairness, storytelling can be hard. As Hollywood screenwriting coach Robert McKee puts it, "Any intelligent person can sit down and make lists. It takes rationality, but little creativity to design an argument using conventional rhetoric. But it demands vivid insight and storytelling skill to present an idea that packs enough emotional power to be memorable."[2]

I've paraphrased four pointers McKee recommends to tell better stories.

▶ Before launching into the current situation, give some background information or history on the company and/or the people involved. Humanize yourself and the organization. Help people relate to you. Talk about why these people, these products, and this company are so meaningful to you.

▶ Share an "inciting incident." This is the thing or things that jarred you awake and made you reexamine "business as usual."

▶ Describe how you're dealing with the inciting incident. How is it making you feel? How do you think you can remedy it? You want to bring out the struggle that you're going through here and make people see it—that's the emotional part that everyone can relate to.

▶ Share the insights you've come to regarding a path forward. How do you think you can pull yourself out of the hole? Or, how *did* you pull yourself out of the hole? What realizations have you come to?

A Word About SWFFs and Morality

More than once, when I've shared the hallmarks of a good organizational SWFF—stirs emotion, story-based, simple, and inspires action—someone has come back with the following type of question or one similar to it.

"Doug, I really like the concept of a SWFF, and the elements ring true to me, but couldn't you argue that leaders who want to do bad things also follow the same formula? For example, I'm sure Enron had a strong SWFF."

Unfortunately, the answer is yes. Stirring emotions and rallying people can be used to do great things, but they can also be used to do bad things. History is filled with examples of both.

There's no simple checklist for a strong moral fiber. That said, I offer four questions that can spark a healthy debate and be used as somewhat of a litmus test.

▶ Do we feel, in our heart of hearts, that what we're doing is right?

▶ Would we be proud to share this SWFF with our family and friends?

▶ Would we be proud to recruit others into this SWFF?

▶ Does this SWFF have a net positive effect on our community and on society?

Taking the time to reflect on these questions and come to a conclusive "yes" is a good indication that you're on the right track.

Chapter 5 Summary

▶ SWFFs in an organization are almost immediately perceptible from the moment you walk in the front door because they tend to pervade everything and everyone.

▶ A good organizational SWFF tends to have four distinguishing characteristics: stirs emotion, story-based, simple, and inspires action.

▶ Menasha Packaging provides an example of a delivered SWFF. With its back against the wall, it did some soul-searching, changing its mindset and its approach to its business—and this had a powerfully positive impact.

▶ The example of the IT group at a global bank shows how a somewhat "under-the-radar" dynamic in an organization can be raised, uncovering a SWFF that drives change.

▶ WisdomTree provides an example of the critical power and importance of a SWFF in entrepreneurial situations, where the odds are often really stacked against success.

▶ Some visions and missions may be SWFFs, but not all of them are. A vision and/or mission is a SWFF only if it's deeply embedded in the organization and—quite simply—inspires people to fight for something.

PART THREE

SEE THE FUTURE NOW

The Future Is All Around You

> The future is already here—it's just not evenly
> distributed.
>
> —**WILLIAM GIBSON,** science fiction writer

You've probably never heard of J.C.R. Licklider, but you owe him a big debt of gratitude.

In 1957, the Soviet Union had just launched Sputnik, demonstrating that it held a lead in missile technology and could conceivably initiate a missile-based nuclear first strike against the United States. The following year, the U.S. Department of Defense formed the Advanced Research Projects Agency (ARPA). Among its first mandates was to develop a reasonable defense to a Soviet first strike.

High on ARPA's list of priorities was ensuring vital communications among various military installations. At the time, communications were relatively unsophisticated and highly centralized. If you took out the central node, the entire system would go down. One of ARPA's goals was to create a communications web where that wouldn't happen.

Here's where Licklider enters the story. A humble, mild-mannered experimental psychologist and MIT professor, Licklider was an improbable technologist. He had no real background in computer engineering, and he came into contact with computers only through a research project on psychoacoustics. He was simply looking to better understand how the human brain and ear convert vibrations into audible sounds. In the late 1950s, Licklider left his position at MIT and joined the research firm Bolt, Beranek and Newman (BBN), where he was given access to one of the more powerful computers of the time.

Through these experiences, Licklider began to realize that computers could play a much larger role in human lives. He described his ideas in a paper titled, "Man-Computer Symbiosis."[1] He saw that humans and computers would form more interactive relationships. This seminal, groundbreaking thought led one technologist of the time to later write, "For the life of me, I could not imagine how a psychologist, who, in 1956, had no apparent knowledge of computers, could have written such a profound and insightful paper about my field in 1960."[2]

In August 1962, Licklider coauthored another paper titled, "On-Line Man-Computer Communication," in which he expanded on his computing ideas, describing how a large number of computers, interconnected to form a geographically and institutionally distributed network, could create an interactive system.[3] Thus Licklider was the first to describe the Internet as we know it today.

By then, ARPA had contracted with BBN. In the fall of 1962, Licklider was named by the director of ARPA to head the Information Processing Techniques Office. His mandate was to bring his vision of networked computers to reality by connecting the geographically distributed computers used by the Department of Defense. As a former academic with strong ties to the world of academe, Licklider directed ARPA funding away from the private sector to researchers at universities such as Stanford, MIT, UCLA, and Berkeley; the early founders and nucleus of the Internet.

Licklider left ARPA two years later. In 1968, he wrote the third of his triumvirate of papers that predicted and laid out the future of computing. In "The Computer as a Communication Device," Licklider argued that the ARPA network was the beginning of a computer-based community.[4] He saw the basis of this community as being the transfer of data, enabling users to interact in meaningful ways. Licklider and his coauthor argued that such a network could, "change the nature and value of communication even more profoundly than did the printing press and the picture tube, for, as we shall show, a well-programmed computer can provide direct access both to informational resources and to the processes for making use of the resources."

Over the course of eight years, Licklider had gone from a quiet and humble experimental psychologist to one of the leading early visionaries behind the development of the modern Internet.[5] What's so uncanny is that he did it surrounded by the same data as many other researchers—and with much less technical expertise.

Licklider's most powerful tools were curiosity and persistence. He allowed himself to ponder big questions that others weren't pondering, even though those questions were right underneath their noses, too. He asked himself a critical question over and over: *What are the possibilities of these things I'm seeing for the future?* His insights evolved over time. Each insight stood on the shoulders of past insights, slowly forming a picture.

Most important, Licklider didn't discount the insights he was having. He didn't think, *What right do I have as a psychologist to be seeing the future of computing?* Instead, he just described the future he saw from his unique perspective. In the process, he foretold one of the most important technological innovations of the twentieth century.

We All Have the Ability to See the Future

When I tell Licklider's story to businesspeople, I often hear a similar response: "That's pretty cool, but he was a researcher who was paid to think about big things on a daily basis. It's easy to do that from the ivory tower of an academic setting. Caught up in my day-to-day responsibilities, it's hard for me to find time to do that kind of thinking."

My response is always threefold. First, many of the greatest innovations of the last century have come from the commercial sector. Second, if you don't take the time to see the future now, someone else will, and you'll then have to try to catch them if you can. Third, you don't have to discover anything as big as the Internet to see the future now. Most of the insights that will have a big impact on your business are right in front of your eyes. You just have to take the time to see them.

Ask Larry Tribble. Over the last 35 years, Tribble has done a great job of seeing the future now.

Tribble is the CEO of Southern Auto Auction (SAA) in East Windsor, Connecticut, the largest independent whole-sale auto auction in the United States. Since taking over at SAA in the late 1970s, he's grown it from a solid local player to a regional powerhouse, primarily through continually asking just one question: "What can we do better?"

SAA currently auctions approximately 4,000 cars a week, all on Wednesday. To handle this volume, he's developed a facility of more than 300 acres with 20 state-of-the-art auction lanes that run like well-oiled machines. The target time for each car through the lane is 45 seconds. It's a number he's very aware of because every second counts. If he can shave 1 second off 4,000 auctions in a day, he can get an additional 40 cars through the lanes. It's a business of numbers.

But Tribble isn't a numbers guy. While he thinks about numbers every day, he's much more comfortable in the world of new ideas. He knows that if he keeps his attention on the big questions, this will drive the numbers. Stemming from the overarching question that's always on his mind (what can we do better?) comes a series of others.

Where will his industry be in 5 or 10 years? What forces will help or hinder it? What are other industries doing that he can learn from? His focus on continuing to ask and find answers to these questions is what drives his ability to see the future now. To do so, he uses a process he calls *search and reapply*. He proactively looks at what's going on outside of his industry and thinks about how it could apply to SAA.

One way he does this is through walkabouts. A walkabout is exactly what it sounds like—getting out of your current environment and walking around somewhere else. Tribble has taken walkabouts all over the world to learn from a wide variety of organizations.

He's spent time at the enormous Dutch flower auctions at Aalsmeer in the Netherlands. Housed in the fourth-largest building in the world, these auctions run every day and generate almost $5 billion a year in revenue. He studied how the auctioneers get highly perishable products in and out quickly using reverse auction techniques. Studying an even more perishable product, he visited the Tokyo wholesale fish auction in Japan, where fish are flown in from around the world overnight and sold the next day. He's also spent time at Ritchie Brothers, watching industrial cranes get auctioned, and at Sotheby's, watching the auctioning of art. From each, he's picked up little ideas on where his industry can go, how to lead it there, and, most important, how to make his customer relationships stronger.

Providing unparalleled customer service is an idea that Tribble got from studying another industry. In addition to going on walkabouts, he loves to read case studies to shake up his thinking. Two hotel studies have always stuck with him: the Four Seasons and Ritz-Carlton.

They left Tribble with a question that drives his customer orientation: "How can we translate the kind of service that five-star hotels provide to our business?" The result is that a visit to SAA can feel more like a day at a country club than a trip to buy or sell cars. The facilities are immaculate, the staff is extremely friendly, and you can even get a pretty decent meal for an auto auction. In an industry that's often bare-bones and transactional, SAA is known as "the gentleman's auction." It's a big reason why customers keep coming back.

Perhaps the biggest payoff from Tribble's inquisitive nature was the technological lead he got over his competition in the early 1990s. After seeing a digital camera for the first time, he started wondering how he could transfer images of cars between sellers and buyers.

A couple of years later, that simple question produced Auction 2000, an inventory management system that allowed fleets to manage their cars at SAA. It was one of the key innovations that catapulted SAA ahead of the competition. It decreased his staff's workload, increased inventory accuracy, and made it easier to do business with SAA. To give you a sense of just how far out in front of the curve Tribble was, he even shipped PCs to customers who didn't yet have them so that they could start using the system. It would be 10 years before his competition was using technology like this in any significant way. Moreover, when the Internet boom hit, he was in a perfect position to take advantage of it because he already had the databases in place to feed his site.

The risks that Tribble took weren't huge or headline-making. They were just the everyday risks of a sharp businessman who was looking at the future all around him, asking straightforward questions, having some critical insights, and placing a few strategic bets on them. When you break it all down, that's the essence of creating a competitive advantage.

Keeping Your Eyes and Ears Open

Great ideas are everywhere. The forces that will have the biggest impact on your life and business in the coming years are all around you. But you have to have your antennae up in order to sense them. Often, brilliant insights are thought to be the result of superior intellect or skill. While those things certainly help, they're not the primary drivers.

What really helps you see the future around you is being more curious, asking more questions, digging a little bit deeper, forming testable hypotheses, and doing those things over and over. Your goal is to decrease uncertainty and increase the propensity for action. That's what Licklider and Tribble did. While their achievements are exceptional, the skills and practices they used are not. They're available to everyone. People and teams who consistently take smart risks do three things to get better at seeing the future now.

> *See the world through your customers' eyes.* What do your customers want? Sometimes they know and you can ask them. Sometimes they don't know and you have to lead them there. Either way, you have to see the world through their eyes to gain clarity and conviction concerning which risks will pay off and which won't.
>
> *Stop, think, discuss, and decide.* When it comes to taking risks, the tendency in most organizations to either miss the boat

or do something really stupid can also be traced to people's inability to think and talk together at critical moments. For all the fancy planning tools these days, stopping and having a thoughtful conversation is still the most powerful tool for gaining clarity about the future. And making clear decisions based on these conversations is the most powerful tool to gain traction to move forward. By employing a few simple decision-making tools, individuals and teams can get better at making good decisions faster.

Predict your fail points. Every plan carries both the seeds of success *and* the seeds of failure. If you don't see possible failures coming, it's hard to head them off. Predicting where something might fail is never comfortable, but it's absolutely necessary when it comes to taking smart risks. Simple questions and a focused team to think about them will usually uncover the vast majority of the fail points you might encounter.

In the next three chapters, I'll walk you through each of these topics in more detail.

IDEAS AND TOOLS FOR ACTION

Go on Walkabouts

As Tribble did, get out of your milieu and go visit other organizations that you admire. This will shake up your thinking and give you great ideas that your competitors probably aren't thinking about. Furthermore, it keeps you from getting stale just sitting around your organization. The following is a suggested approach. I recommend doing it once every year or two, if not more often.

1. Make a short list of leaders and/or organizations that you've admired over the last few years. Be sure to include people in tangential positions and in different industries from yours.

2. Under each entry, clarify specifically what it is you admire about this person or organization and what it's been able to accomplish.

3. Pick one or two that you'd like to know more about. These are possible targets for a walkabout. If you want to keep the visit short and sweet, choose people or organizations in or around your area. If you're up for travel, broaden the list.

4. Sometimes you can visit the organization without an invitation. However, that's not always possible, so you have to plan ahead. Either way, reach out to the leader you admire, explain the exercise, ask to chat with him, and get a tour if appropriate. In general, people are extremely flattered by the idea.

5. After the visit, codify one to three lessons learned, clarifying the implications for your business and possible new directions you can take.

Network like a Journalist

While you can't go on walkabouts every week or every month, you can network that often. Many people network, but the majority of them don't make the most of it. They leave no smarter than when they came in. They engage in a series of "what do you do?" conversations that go only an inch deep. Little to no value is created.

Use networking opportunities to really dig into someone else's thinking. Like a journalist, look for insights that people are having about the world. Try to leave smarter. Here are some of my favorite questions to ask. With each, keep probing people's answers to see if you can find useful insights they're having:

1. What are the biggest challenges you're seeing in your business?

2. What are the biggest opportunities you're seeing in your business?

3. What's been most surprising to you over the last couple of years?

4. What are you most hopeful about?
5. What are you most concerned about?

In addition to leaving smarter, what's great about this approach is that it's more enjoyable for both parties because the conversations feel more substantive.

Read More

This pretty much speaks for itself. The only reason I've included it is that when life's too busy, it's one of the first things to drop off our to-do lists. If you can read the newspaper cover to cover each day, that's great. If you can read only an article or two a day, that's also good. The bottom line is that it's helpful to get ideas and perspectives regularly from outside of your own bailiwick and thinking.

Our minds tend to process ideas in the background as we go about our lives. One day, weeks later, we'll be reading something and suddenly realize that its theme is similar to those of two other articles we read before. We'll notice a pattern. Often you can make connections that others aren't making because no one article has the whole insight. If you do this enough, you'll start to see the future trends affecting your business that will tee up conversations about new possibilities.

Chapter 6 Summary

▶ The future is all around you, but it's easy to miss. You have to stop, look around, and ask questions in order to see it.

▶ Curiosity is king. If you're not curious about a particular problem or issue, you'll seldom see the future.

▶ Don't discount the insights you're having about the future. Very often you're the only one with your unique set of experiences who's seeing something—and maybe the only one having that particular insight.

▶ Even if others are having similar insights, they may not realize the importance of these insights and therefore may not do anything about them.

► You don't have to see the future with complete clarity in the
  beginning. It usually takes time to unfold. The more you move
  forward, the clearer it gets. Persistence is key.
► The future that you see doesn't have to be earth-shattering.
  Great ideas are often the result of relatively simple insights.
► Simple things like walkabouts, networking like a journalist, and
  reading more can have a profound impact on your ability to
  see the future if you keep your eyes and ears open.

See the World Through Your Customers' Eyes

Winners invent and live by a process of customer learning and discovery.

—STEVEN BLANK, *Four Steps to the Epiphany*

Custom injection molders make plastic parts for just about everything you use, from controls in cars to keys on computers. Reactive in nature, these companies work on thin margins and are subject to the whims of their customers.

For years, running a custom injection-molding company was pretty straightforward. You landed a few large customers— say automakers—and then churned out parts for them for as long they would let you. Your customers dictated how you ran your business, from processes to pricing to payment terms. Your main point of contact was a low-level purchasing manager whose job was to constantly beat you up on price. While this was frustrating, you took the beatings because there were thousands of competitors ready to take your place if you balked. It wasn't a particularly sexy or attractive industry, but it paid the bills.

Those were the good old days.

Now, with so much manufacturing taking place overseas, the molding business in the United States has gotten tougher. Eight thousand custom injection molders are all fighting for a smaller and smaller piece of a shrinking pie. These days, it's considered a win if you can even *find* a low-level purchasing manager to beat you up. A tough business has gotten *brutal*.

But you wouldn't guess it if you walked into Thogus Products Company, a custom injection molder in Cleveland, Ohio. Whiteboards full of big ideas are everywhere. Twenty- to thirty-year-olds race around with a sense of purpose and energy. If it weren't for the millions of dollars of manufacturing equipment, you'd think you'd entered a Silicon Valley start-up. Thogus is a far cry from your father's or grandfather's Rust Belt.

Matt Hlavin, CEO of Thogus, calls it the New Industrial Revolution. Instead of just churning out parts, he's adding high-value services that support the manufacturing process. Thogus now provides design, development, and rapid prototyping services that used to be the purview of his customers' R&D organizations. This has allowed Thogus to move up the food chain into more strategic conversations.

While successful now, this was a risky proposition when Hlavin started adding these services in 2009. In the middle of a recession, Hlavin's company, like many others, was in a decline. It was going to take significant start-up capital to get these services going. Moreover, Hlavin had never delivered these services before and had no idea what he was getting his company into.

But in the face of big obstacles, Hlavin pushed forward anyway. Where did he find the confidence?

He credits the time he spent with his customers.

As the recession deepened, Hlavin listened more and more to his customers' talk about their challenges. Budgets were tight and showed no signs of loosening. Laid-off design and engineering positions weren't coming back, unlike in previous recessions. Everyone was having to do more with less. Teams were getting burned out. Fear and anxiety were rampant.

As Hlavin describes it, "These were big, game-changing problems for our customers, and no one was helping them solve them in a beginning-to-end, cost-effective way. I realized there was a 'blue ocean' market opportunity to help current and new customers become more efficient, while simultaneously improving quality. I heard these challenges so often that I became convinced that if I built a suite of services to address them, people would come."

Over the next couple of years, Hlavin invested more than $2 million in rapid prototyping equipment that typically only large manufacturers like GE and Boeing buy. He also purchased a design firm and kept hiring as his competitors were continuing to let people go.

In the beginning, others thought he was crazy. But by 2011, it was clear that Hlavin had made smart moves. As he had predicted, customers saw the value of his new services and started to buy.

"We can design, prototype, and test things very quickly here," one customer noted. "Furthermore, because these guys build their manufacturing knowledge into the design phase, we don't end up with pretty concepts that are unmanufacturable. When it's time to mass-produce, we can hit the ground running. Thogus's end-to-end approach is a great idea."

Of course it is. After all, it was Hlavin's customers who had given it to him.

Spending More Time with Customers

Sometimes the most powerful business advice is the simplest.

What Matt Hlavin did wasn't rocket science. He spent time with customers and listened to them—a lot. He didn't ask them for specifics on what they wanted; he just started to see the world through their eyes. This is an important distinction, because customers often can't tell you what they really want. They don't really know until they see it. That means you just have to spend enough time with them to be able to start to discern it.

Businesspeople give a lot of excuses for not spending enough time with customers. Being too busy is the most common one I hear. Whenever an executive tells me that she'd love to spend more time with her customers, but she's too busy, I ask to see her calendar for the coming month. Invariably, 50 to 70 percent of what's scheduled could easily be considered lower priority than spending time with important customers. These people just aren't *carving out* the time.

No one knows this better than customer experience expert and bestselling author Tom Connellan.[1] One of the most powerful tools he uses with clients is the customer panel. He puts his client executives in a room with their largest customers so that the customers can give the executives feedback. He asks the customers to share the good, the bad, and the ugly—and not to pull any punches.

Having done hundreds of these panels, Connellan has noticed two overwhelming trends. One, the senior executives are always shocked and surprised by what they hear. Two, the shocking stuff is never good.

One of his best stories is of a defense contractor who brought in a U.S. Navy admiral as one of its customers. Before the admiral even sat down, everyone could tell that he was in a foul mood. When it was his turn to speak, he launched right in, wasting no time with pleasantries.

"How many of you have ever been on one of my boats?" the admiral asked loudly and sternly.

None of the executives' hands went up. The admiral surveyed the room for a few seconds and then remarked in a scolding tone, "I didn't think so."

Connellan could see the executives straightening up in their chairs.

"How many of you have ever been with any of my sailors?" the admiral followed up.

Again, none of the executives' hands went up.

The admiral surveyed the room another time for effect, seemingly meeting the eyes of every single executive before saying, "I didn't think so."

"The U.S. Navy is one of your largest customers," the admiral continued, "and yet none of you has ever been on one of my boats and none of you has ever spent any time with my sailors."

For the next 10 minutes, the admiral went through a list of issues he had with the company. The headline was, the company was totally out of touch with the Navy's needs. He made the point that one product in particular seemed to have been developed with absolutely *zero* knowledge of what a sailor does on a daily basis.

He finished by saying, "You're so busy trying to sell me 'stuff' that you've forgotten that I have customers, and those are the men and women out in the fleet that are defending our country right now. If they're happy, I'm happy. If they're not happy, I'm not happy. You have to stop spending time schmoozing me and start spending time figuring out what *they* need."

Connellan has so many stories like this that it's scary. It's an endemic problem throughout many organizations. Leaders at all levels don't get out of the office and don't have their eyes and ears on the street. Instead, they see the world through the hazy fog of their conference rooms and boardrooms. Layers of other people, who aren't getting out of the office either, are advising them. It's an organization-wide replication of the classic game of telephone. When it comes time to place bets on the future, these leaders are flying blind, totally out of touch with the nuances of what customers *really* want.

Taking the time to fill in those blind spots leads to decidedly smarter decisions.

The Hedge Fund Manager Who Wouldn't Go out of Network

After failing at his first start-up six years earlier, Cyrus Massoumi knew all too well the pitfalls of not spending enough time seeing the world through his customers' eyes. Slight miscalculations in timing and product had left him with his first entrepreneurial battle scar. While he knew that there were a lot of ways to fail at his new company, ZocDoc, he vowed that it wouldn't be because he didn't understand the true motivations of his customers.

Massoumi and his cofounders interviewed everyone and anyone they could get their hands on before deciding to build ZocDoc, which allows patients to find doctors and schedule appointments with them online. They spoke to all kinds of patients who would be using the service and all kinds of doctors who would be paying for it. In the process, Massoumi and his fellow entrepreneurs got kicked out of quite a few doctors' offices.

"It was an uncomfortable experience, but it was critical to helping us get our pitch right," Massoumi explained. "Every time we got kicked out of another office, it was another lesson learned."

One of their most important lessons came from a potential patient/user—a wealthy hedge fund manager. After an extensive in-depth interview, the hedge fund manager said he thought the service sounded compelling and pointed out a few great benefits, but then he said he'd never use it. His sticking point was that the website wasn't searchable by insurance carrier, and that he couldn't afford to go out of network.

Massoumi thought this was an odd response for someone making millions of dollars a year. So he probed further. After all, the difference in the co-pay price was peanuts to someone like this guy.

"It's not about the price. I can't afford the paperwork," Massoumi recalls the man answering. "I'm deathly afraid of the hoops insurance companies are going to make me jump through to get reimbursed if I go out of network."

Subsequent to that interview, Massoumi asked every other interviewee whether she'd use the service without insurance search functionality. The answer was a resounding "no."

"Had we not gotten that insight right, we would have completely missed the boat," Massoumi said. "That one missing piece would have prevented us from building our user base fast enough to get out of the gates. It was a small insight, but an unbelievably important one."

In retrospect, it seems obvious, but at the time that information led to an about-face in ZocDoc's strategy.

Up until that point, Massoumi had been primarily focused on trying to get doctors on board. His original thinking was that his system would allow users to go out of network. Thus, ZocDoc would help doctors bring in higher-paying out-of-network patients. It was a smart pitch if you're trying to get technophobic, change-weary doctors to buy in. But it was only half the story. Patients were the other half; they also needed a clear value proposition.

What made the insurance search requirement hard to see was Massoumi's personal experience—and how he had originally conceived the company.

"I came up with the idea for ZocDoc after I popped my eardrum on a flight from Seattle to New York and couldn't find an ENT doctor. I didn't care about being out of network. I cared about getting my hearing back," Massoumi explained. "Also, at the time, I was still at my job at McKinsey, and it had excellent out-of-network benefits, so I wasn't so concerned. What was easy to forget was that neither of those things is the average experience of someone who is looking for a doctor."

It's an instructive insight regarding how blind spots can be so easily missed.

Opening Paint Stores in a Recession

Thogus and ZocDoc are examples of how new customer insights can increase the chances of success. Sherwin-Williams is an example of how a 146-year-old mentality and 20-year-old insight can do the same thing.

Sherwin-Williams knows what moves paint—great service and a deep understanding of its customers' needs. Ever since the company invented ready-to-use paint in the late 1800s, it has been obsessed with finding ways to make its customers' lives easier. Talk to anyone at the company today and he'll tell you that Sherwin-Williams considers itself more of a service company than a product company.

"For us, the logic is simple," says Bob Wells, SVP of communications. "There are limited ways to differentiate products in a mature industry like paint. However, there are infinite ways to differentiate on service. Furthermore, great service is harder to replicate, so it's a competitive advantage. The customer is at the forefront of everything we do."

One thing the company spends a lot of time doing is trying to understand painting contractors, who provide 85 percent of its sales. In the early 1990s, after surveying contractors, the company realized something important: contractors often make paint-buying decisions based not on brand of paint but on the proximity of a paint store to their current job. Wells summed it up this way, "In the painting business, time is money. Contractors get tired of driving past three of our competitors' stores on their way to ours. If we're not close to their current job, they often switch brands."

This insight led to a hypothesis. If Sherwin-Williams saturated a market with stores, its share of contractor business in that market would grow faster than its number of stores. The reasoning was simple: stores would be closer to more jobs, so contractors would start switching to Sherwin-Williams. Then the contractors would stick with Sherwin-Williams because its stores would be convenient to just about any job.

The company tested its hypothesis in Houston, Dallas, Atlanta, and Cleveland—and it worked. When the store count in these markets doubled, revenue *more than doubled*, creating a network effect. Contractors could find Sherwin-Williams everywhere. New stores got to profitability faster, and current store revenues also increased.

Once its initial experiment worked, Sherwin-Williams began implementing it in other markets. But competitors quickly caught on. Before long, it became a foot race for prime real estate. "We'd put in a store, and a few months later a competitor's store would pop up across the street," Wells said. "It made it tough to get an outsized advantage. This neck-and-neck race is how it's been for the last 20 years."

Enter the recession of 2008.

With revenue down across the industry, there was a lot of pressure to cut costs. One of the easiest ways to do it was to close stores. So that's exactly what Sherwin-Williams's competitors did; they shuttered low-performing stores and all but stopped new store openings.

Sherwin-Williams did just the opposite.

It saw the recession as a golden opportunity to get prime real estate uncontested. Doubling down, the company kept opening 60 to 100 stores a year while its closest competitor opened 12. Expenses increased and revenues dropped. Shareholders pushed back hard, but Sherwin-Williams stood its ground. It knew that the market would bounce back eventually, and it didn't want to miss a rare opportunity to position itself for the future of its customers' business.

Now, four years later, it looks as if Sherwin-Williams made a smart bet. On strong sales, particularly in 2011 and 2012, its stock price has nearly tripled since 2009, and its revenue growth has far surpassed its competitors'.

When I asked Wells how the company found the conviction to make such a contrarian bet, to push back against shareholders who were maniacally focused on quarterly performance metrics, he didn't have an easy answer. Instead, he waxed philosophical.

"We've always looked at business more like dating than like war. It's a theme that runs through our 146-year history. In war, you're focused on beating the competition. In dating, you're focused on strengthening a relationship. That difference of perspective has a million knock-on effects for how decisions get made. One of those decisions was to position ourselves to better serve our customers when the recession ended."

Wells's last comment is telling. More than a set of disconnected actions, seeing the world through your customers' eyes is a mindset that informs everything you do.

IDEAS AND TOOLS FOR ACTION

Traditional market research methods, such as formal surveys, focus groups, and analyzing usage and buying patterns, are great ways to take the pulse of your customers. They identify broad themes about strengths, weaknesses, and areas for growth. This kind of data opens your eyes to dynamics you've been missing and points to opportunities you can take advantage of. Sherwin-Williams did a great job of this.

Beyond traditional market research methods, however, it's important to add more informal interactions with customers or clients that can bring more nuanced insights to the surface. That's how Hlavin and Massoumi got some of their most important ideas.

There are hundreds of ways to do this. The following are three simple, yet powerful customer activities.

Eat with Your Customers More Often

Breaking bread is a great way to open up conversations and get thinking flowing. Unfortunately, fewer and fewer people take the time to do it these days.

At a minimum, take a key customer out to breakfast, lunch, or dinner every two to four weeks. Your goal is to understand the biggest issues on your customers' minds. What are they excited about or worried about? What do they see coming down the road in the future?

Your role is to listen, understand, and troubleshoot if appropriate. In general, you need to be a sounding board. Become a valuable thought partner.

Obviously some clients will be more receptive to this than others, so go where the energy is. The more you dine with your customers, the easier it becomes and the more valuable a resource you become. You also start to see more important angles and patterns that you miss when you're sitting in your office.

Go Out on *Learning* Calls

Everyone does sales calls. Few people do learning calls.

Like the walkabouts discussed in Chapter 6, learning calls can be an invaluable source of revelation. When walking the halls at a customer's site, you see interesting things that your customers never tell you—ways in which they're using your products or services; specific issues they have that they don't realize.

Learning calls are easy to set up. Customers tend to be receptive to having you come in and learn more about their business or watch them in action. Also, your presence gives a strong message that you really care about specifics and helping them solve problems. Here are a few pointers that help:

1. Explain to your customer what you'd like to get out of the exercise—for example, you want to chat about how service is going, get a tour of key facilities, and meet with a few key players if possible.
2. Don't mix your learning visit with a sales call. Be clear about this with your customer. Do much more listening than talking.
3. After the visit, codify one to three lessons learned, clarifying the implications for your business and possible new directions to take.

Do "What I'm Seeing and Hearing" Reports

The last two suggestions play better in a business-to-business than in a business-to-consumer environment. You can do the following exercise anywhere. At the end of each week, have key employees around the company forward "what I'm seeing and hearing" reports. These are informal, three- to five-bullet-point summaries of things they've noticed over the past week that others around the company might be interested in hearing. To make the reports more effective:

1. Pick a specific question you'd like people to answer or a sentence to complete. For example, "Something interesting I noticed this week was . . . ," or, "In my conversations with customers this week I learned. . . ."
2. Have people keep it short and sweet, sharing it by e-mail.
3. Once a month, have someone summarize the themes he sees and send those around, too.

What you'll see over time is that themes will work in the background of people's thinking. They'll start seeing themes they hadn't noticed before merely because other people are mentioning them. Examples might be customer interest, lack of interest, or new problems that aren't on anyone's radar yet. These then help inform future directions for your organization.

Chapter 7 Summary

► Seeing the world through your customers' eyes increases your propensity to act because it decreases your uncertainty about the future. You're hearing your customers' issues over and over again, gaining important insights about what they want and need.

► Seeing the world through your customers' eyes is different from asking your customers what they want or need. Very often customers can't put into words what they want and need. That's why you have to look through their eyes to see it.

► The most important thing you can do to see the world through your customers' eyes is to spend more time with them.

► It's common to think that being out of touch with your customers happens more at Fortune 500 companies. This isn't true. Large, medium, and small companies are all equal-opportunity offenders.

► Rather than a set of one-time actions, seeing the world through your customers' eyes should be a mindset that's baked into everything you do. From internal meetings to external meetings to reading the news every day, you should always be asking yourself, "What are the implications here for our customers?"

Stop, Think, Discuss, and Decide

Most organizations' problems can be traced to their inability to think and talk together at critical moments.

—WILLIAM ISAACS (PARAPHRASED), *Dialogue: The Art of Thinking Together*

The future never reveals itself in a set of clear implications and stepwise plans of action. If it did, it wouldn't be risk taking, it would be sure-thing taking.

As the future unfolds around us, we have to stop to make sense of it regularly. In the beginning, the process is exploratory. We have a set of hints and gut senses, inklings and random thoughts. Often it must stay that way for a while, as the best ideas start off a little harebrained. We immerse ourselves in them, discussing and exploring them in order to understand the many forces that are at play and their implications. We can't rush this process or we risk coming to the wrong conclusions.

At the same time, we can't take forever. There will always be unknowables. Eventually, we have to make choices, even though uncertainty never completely goes away. It's the only way to give ourselves a shot at success.

Seeing the future now is all about managing the tension between opening doors for exploration and closing them for action.

The Power of Focusing on a Clear End State

When you're pursuing a difficult and risky course of action, there's a pervasive illusion that the more doors you leave open, the greater your chances of success. You think you have more options this way. In practice, I've found it's just the opposite. The more doors you *close*, the greater your chances of success.[1] It comes down to the power of focus and a clear end state. When you leave too many doors open, you scatter your energy, which often results in disastrous consequences.

From 1910 to 1912, in the middle of the Heroic Age of Antarctic Exploration, one of the most dramatic narratives of that 25-year period played out between explorers Robert F. Scott of Great Britain and Roald Amundsen of Norway. Leading separate expeditions, they were simultaneously trying to become the first to reach the South Pole—one of the last great exploration prizes on earth. The story is so memorable that the American Museum of Natural History had a four-month exhibit in 2010 commemorating the 100-year anniversary of the events, titled "Race to the End of the Earth," which I visited several times.[2]

On paper, Scott clearly had the advantage. He had a two-month head start leaving Europe, he had explored the Antarctic previously, and he had an edge in financing and provisions. As well, he had a team of experienced explorers with a range of skills specifically designed to support a push to the pole.

And yet, in February 1912, as Amundsen announced his expedition's success from his quarters in Australia, Scott was foundering on the ice and snow of Antarctica. A month later, Scott and his four-man polar team lay dying of cold and lack of food. His final agony was the knowledge that Amundsen had beaten him to the pole by 33 days.

The reasons Amundsen succeeded so spectacularly, while Scott met with abysmal tragedy, have fascinated historians for the last century. A few historians have heralded Scott as a hero who merely met with unlucky circumstances. Others have painted him as a bungler with poor foresight and bad character judgment. As with all things in life, the truth probably lies somewhere in the murky middle.

However, one thing did become clear to me as I walked through the exhibit. A significant factor contributing to Scott's failure was his lack of focus. In addition to wanting to reach the pole, Scott also had an ambitious scientific agenda for his trip to Antarctica. Much of his team's time was focused on other things, such as geologic, biologic, and oceanographic experiments. That meant that Scott outfitted his ship, chose his men, and chose his modes of transport to meet both of these complex needs. By design, distractions from reaching the South Pole were built into his expedition from the beginning, all of which increased his chances of failure.

Conversely, Amundsen was singularly and maniacally focused on reaching the pole—and that was it. He left nothing to chance in that pursuit. Amundsen chose only highly effective and snow-tested dogs for transport, while Scott brought ineffective ponies and experimental motorized sledges that didn't work. Amundsen began his expedition as soon as the winter broke to get a jump start on reaching the pole, while Scott waited an extra couple of weeks to leave his base camp. Amundsen took a new, shorter route, while Scott took a longer route that had failed in the past.

We'll never know exactly what happened in those fateful months between October 1911 and March 1912, but if my experience working with leaders taking risks is any indication, Amundsen had a decisiveness advantage, that is, he could make decisions faster than Scott. Some of it may have been due to Amundsen's character, but much of it was probably due to the fact that he wasn't trying to accomplish too many goals at once. He had a lean team, all focused on the same thing. When he faced a tough decision, he made it based on only one criterion: would it or would it not help his team get to the South Pole and back safely? He could see the future more clearly because he was focused on only one future. And as a result, he could make decisions faster. Scott's bloated agenda didn't allow for any of these advantages.

Recently, Edward J. Larson wrote in *An Empire of Ice* that Scott was really the greater success because of the research he accomplished.[3] He adds that reaching the South Pole was nothing more than a spectacular sideshow.

To me, that last statement is preposterous. To treat one of the riskiest treks on earth as a sideshow is merely more evidence of Scott's ultimate failing. Scott was unfocused. The seeds of his failure had probably been sown years before, back in Great Britain, when he was gathering his team and resources to try to accomplish too many things.

Shifting the Focus of a Successful Software Company

Amundsen and Scott's fates came down to the decisions they made. In my work with clients, I've never found a foolproof method for making tough decisions—for the simple reason that such a method doesn't exist. What I have found, however, is that having focused strategic conversations on a regular basis goes a long way toward decreasing uncertainty, clarifying a path, and getting everyone aligned around a decision to move forward.

Cyrus Innovation is a 40-person software development company in New York City. In 2010, its business was building software for clients. It was good at it, and it had a great name in the business.

At the same time, the leaders of the company were hungry for a change. While they liked their consulting business, several members of the management team were toying with the idea of pursuing a software product of their own. However, there wasn't a shared commitment to it among the leadership.

Some of the leaders questioned the company's market knowledge: Did it know the right opportunities to pursue, and if not, how would it find them? Some questioned the financial viability: Could the company afford to fund the needed resources to properly pursue a product strategy? Still others questioned the timing: Even if it was a good idea to pursue its own products, was this the right time to do it?

For more than a year, the leaders discussed these ideas in an ad hoc fashion, over lunches and between meetings. Usually the conversations were one-on-one, with someone sharing a few random musings before running off to do something else.

By the summer of 2010, the leaders realized that they'd never get enough clarity and alignment to move forward without having a focused and direct conversation about the topic. Over five days between July and September 2010, they had a series of full-day meetings to explore their possible strategic directions.

At those meetings, the six leaders shared their personal visions for the company and what a product focus would mean to them. They each talked about critical success factors that they saw and probed their colleagues' thinking on the topic. They raised questions and concerns and took the time to explore and discuss them.

By Labor Day, they were all aligned on the idea that focusing on a product strategy was the right thing to do. They defined a big goal: to generate all their revenue from products that they controlled within five years. To achieve that, they decided that they were going to have two of the six leaders focus on product development and invest several developers in supporting those efforts. The other four leaders would continue to serve their consulting clients as a support mechanism. The team would check in every three to six months to reassess the situation and make changes to the strategy as needed.

At the end of those planning meetings, the shift in energy was profound. The leaders felt clear and focused. Knowing where they were headed and being clear on the roles they needed to play, they were excited and felt less hesitant to act. As they shared the plans around the organization, others also became excited.

At the same time, the leaders at Cyrus were clear that what they were trying to do wasn't easy. They anticipated challenges and did not enter the initiative with a Pollyannaish attitude. They knew it was going to take a lot of effort and a little luck. But they also knew that without their newly generated clarity and focus, they wouldn't have found the collective conviction to move forward in the first place.

In September 2010, Rex Madden, one of the Cyrus partners, summed up the three months of planning. "The value of the process wasn't in generating new ideas. Most of what we discussed we'd all been thinking about for years. The value was in getting aligned behind the ideas. We weren't taking the time to stop, think, and talk about them together—and really challenge each other's thinking. Once we did, we were able to prioritize the ideas, and the path forward became clear pretty quickly."

Fast-forward 18 months to March 2012 and the planning they did is still an invaluable beacon.

"The clarity that we generated over that period still guides us," Madden recently shared. "We haven't hit any home runs yet, but we still have two guys focused on products. We're still committed to that path. And we're still convinced we will make this happen. What's interesting, and something we didn't expect, is that our consulting business has really taken off since we did the planning. Our desire to support the new product vision has gotten everyone more energized and focused on our current core business."

Cyrus Innovation's experience illustrates two important points regarding stopping, thinking, and discussing things in an effort to see the future. The first is the importance of getting thinking out on the table in a structured way. The ideas that would shape their future were already percolating in the team members' minds; they'd just never explored them in a cohesive way. Coming together created a whole picture from a variety of perspectives.

Second, the planning process can have positive unintended consequences. A series of meetings to discuss their product opportunities actually strengthened their consulting business. Aligning on a product vision made them realize what consulting had to do to successfully support the business.

120 Whispers Become a Roar That Transforms a Business

Stopping to think deeply about and discuss business strategy is often considered the purview of senior leaders. For many decisions, like Cyrus Innovation's, that's appropriate. However, this next example shows just how powerful it can be to include a much wider group.

In January 2011, at its annual teamwide offsite, the insurance management team (IMT) at kidney dialysis provider DaVita took the time to stop and explore a simple question: *How can we have more proactive and productive conversations with our patients?*

IMT's role at DaVita is to help patients navigate the tricky world of insurance to ensure that patients receive education on the optimal insurance coverage for their healthcare needs. For example, a sick patient who doesn't understand his insurance options might struggle to take public transportation to dialysis three times a week, when his insurance would actually cover home pickup. IMT wants to make sure that situations like this don't happen.

"We were doing a good job of helping patients retain insurance coverage," said Cassie Cone, VP of IMT, "but we wanted to ensure that patients also had help finding the best insurance coverage for them. We wanted to be more proactive in our patient support. On the one hand, being more proactive helps DaVita get reimbursed for services provided. More important, though, it helps patients improve their quality of life. It's a win-win."

In four small group breakout sessions, every member of the 120-person team weighed in on the question at hand. Going into the sessions, the management team thought that the group would uncover a few good insights regarding incremental changes the company could make to its current processes. Coming out of the sessions, the team members realized that they had an opportunity to vastly improve their customer service by restructuring their entire department.

The idea of making bold decisions by taking time to think through pressing issues together is nothing new for DaVita.

Nearly bankrupt and at death's door in 1999, DaVita's tremendous turnaround, led by CEO Kent Thiry, has been the subject of many books and business school cases. At the core of the story is DaVita's culture of community and caring. One of the benefits of its culture is that it promotes opportunities for robust dialogue between the teammates who are working hands-on with patients. This was evident in IMT's 2011 meeting.

"There were two big differences between the January 2011 meeting and our prior annual meetings," Cone reflected. "First, previous meetings had been at the end of the year and had had a decidedly 'look back' feel to them. Because we moved the 2011 meeting to January, people were eager to look forward. Second, we were intentional about giving everyone on the team a voice. While we have a culture that supports open communication, we had traditionally packed our meeting agenda full of content. This historical approach didn't allow us to capture teammates' ideas on how we could improve. Looking forward, and facilitating small group discussions on how we could better serve our customer, is what gave us the game-changing idea at this meeting."

In brief, the game-changing insight was that IMT could become more effective by combining existing roles and reducing the number of patients each teammate served—a significant restructuring.

"It made a lot of sense, but it didn't seem practical at first," shared Jud Dean, director of IMT. "To make the idea work, we were going to have to increase our headcount by about 60 percent in the middle of a recession, redistribute our existing teammates, and retrain everyone. These are hardly simple things to execute. However, as all of us on the management team heard the dialogue get louder and become a roar, we realized that we had to find a way to make some big changes."

Within weeks, the IMT management team met to explore options. The managers knew they couldn't just ask for the budget to hire 70 more people. They would have to show that, in addition to providing improved patient support, the larger operation could also support itself financially. They concluded that the best way to do this was to bootstrap a pilot that could clearly demonstrate both quality and financial improvements.

Two teams volunteered, one in Florida and one in Maryland. Six teammates were chosen for the pilot from April to October 2011. Another 30 teammates were added from October to December. During that time, colleagues from outside the pilot had to pick up the slack in the pilot employees' workload. To reduce risk, no new employees could be added until the pilot was deemed a success.

"It was a risky proposition. We were redrafting roles and responsibilities. Some people liked it, and some people didn't. The biggest help in getting over hurdles was the fact that everyone felt ownership of the decision because all their voices had helped drive it," Dean said.

Amazingly, by December 2011, with only 25 percent of its workforce piloting the new methods, IMT had already created double the financial gain needed to justify adding the 70 new employees. The new hires were built into the 2012 budget, not even a year after the seemingly crazy idea first surfaced.

"There are a lot of lessons that I take away from the experience," Dean said. "One of the most significant is how much clarity, focus, and momentum come from having a good, inclusive dialogue at the beginning of a process. First of all, we wouldn't have come up with the idea if we hadn't engaged the entire team. Second, even if we had somehow come up with the idea on our own, we wouldn't have had the whole team behind us the way we did. And that's what made it such a success."

IDEAS AND TOOLS FOR ACTION

The title of this chapter says it all—stop, think, discuss, and decide. If you've got something that's worth fighting for, you're taking the time to look at the future, and you're doing your research with customers and others, the only thing left to do is sort through the insights you've gathered and make a choice. This is the "final mile" of seeing the future now. In many ways, it's the most significant mile because without it, decisions don't get teed-up and made.

The following are some ideas and tools for action focusing on the two places where I see leaders and teams struggling the most in stopping, thinking, discussing, and deciding: (1) failure to get thinking out on the table for everyone to see, understand, and discuss, and (2) failure to close doors and come to a focused decision.

Get Thinking Out on the Table

It's easy to find reasons for not bringing thinking to the surface. You're too busy. You're not sure whether what you're thinking about is a good or a valid idea. You haven't really formed a strong opinion about it yet. You don't know if it's important. You're not really sure where to start.

However, the problem with not getting thinking out on the table is that it never gets the chance to grow and develop. Ideas tend to mature in the outside world, when you give voice to them. They meet and integrate with other people's ideas to gain strength. If you keep ideas to yourself, they stay small and weak.

Sometimes getting thinking out on the table can happen through a simple brainstorming session. Sometimes it takes more personal reflection in advance. As a general rule, I tell my clients that if they're not taking at least 60 minutes a week to stop and think about the big picture, there's no way they'll ever be able to see the future now. They'll simply be too caught up in the day-to-day details. Following are a few suggestions for exercising the muscle of getting thinking out on the table.

Do Sentence-Stem Completions

Some people are naturally gifted at sitting down and thinking about the future. For others, it's more of a chore. When it's difficult, I recommend using a tool called sentence-stem completion. It's a deceptively simple exercise. Merely finish the end of a sentence stem several times or more. This can be done alone or in a group.

Instructions for Sentence-Stem Completion

1. Complete the end of one or more of the following sentence stems.
2. Don't think too much. Do it quickly in a stream of consciousness. You're trying to tap into what's already there, but is not yet top of mind for you.
3. You can use as little as a few words or as much as a paragraph. The most important thing is that you get your mind flowing and your ideas out.
4. Complete each sentence at least *five to ten times*. Each completion taps into a new train of thought.

Sample "See the Future Now" Sentence Stems

▶ *The most important things I/we can focus on in the next two years are . . .*
▶ *Currently, I think I'm/we're missing an opportunity to . . .*
▶ *Something I think I/we could and should be much better at is . . .*
▶ *Something I believe I/we need to know more about is . . .*
▶ *As I look back over the last few years, what's most surprising to me is . . .*

As you complete one or more of these sentences, begin to notice where you see themes. What's new information to you? What have you seen many times before? Where do your convictions feel stronger? Where do things seem to be more than just a good idea and worth pursuing?

Answer Key Strategic Questions

Completing strategic sentence stems is a broad brainstorming process. Identifying and answering key strategic questions is more narrowly focused on the important drivers of your business. In an organizational setting, identifying key strategic questions help ensure that everyone stays on the same page as things invariably shift and move.

Sam Palmisano, the recently retired CEO of IBM, attributes the company's strong performance over the last decade to its ability to get everyone focused on key strategic questions. He developed four questions that guided every strategic decision the company made. Steve Lohr shared the questions and Palmisano's thinking behind them in a December 2011 *New York Times* article.[4]

The four questions are:

1. "Why would someone spend their money with you—so what is unique about you?"
2. "Why would somebody work for you?"
3. "Why would society allow you to operate in their defined geography—their country?"
4. "And why would somebody invest their money with you?"

Lohr reported that Palmisano found that the questions were a great way to "focus thinking and prod the company beyond its comfort zone and to make I.B.M. pre-eminent again. . . . The pursuit of excellence in those four dimensions shaped the strategy."

Palmisano's questions are a great example of the type and level of questions you want. You can imagine that the answers to those questions will point to the essence of what will make IBM successful. I recommend using them as a model and tweaking and changing them for your business as needed.

Prioritize Everyone's Thinking

Once you've gotten thinking on the table, whether through sentence stems, key strategic questions, or another brainstorming process, prioritization is an important next step in order to narrow options. Often these are some of the most interesting conversations because this process forces people to make choices that they don't normally think about.

There are a lot of prioritization techniques. One of the most straightforward is voting. Let's say a team of eight people has generated 20 ideas about the path forward on a given issue. All of the ideas are interesting in some way. First, the team should decide what decision criteria should drive voting. Examples include expected return, ease of implementation, and level of interest. Each person is then given 3 votes. In this example, that would mean a total of 24 votes in the room. Each person votes for his top three choices based on the criteria the team aligned on.

Once the voting is complete, the team should prioritize the list by vote tally and debrief the outcome. Did some things obviously rise to the top? Did some things fall off the list? Are there three to five items with highest priorities to discuss further?

Come to a Focused Decision

You've gotten your thinking out on the table, discussed it, and prioritized it. Unfortunately, as is always the case in life, things might still be unclear to some degree. However, you have to make a decision because, as we saw in the Scott Antarctic example at the beginning of the chapter, leaving too many options on the table can have disastrous consequences. If you have too many options, you will rarely generate the focus and momentum needed to succeed in risky situations.

This is the place where individuals and teams fall down most. In fact, nearly every call I get to help a struggling team centers around this very topic—the inability to come to clear, aligned decisions on important issues. Research by social psychologist Roy Baumeister has shown how tiring it is to decide, especially if you're making hard decisions.[5] Decision fatigue is a far bigger problem these days than most people realize.

Something that's helpful in decreasing the likelihood of decision fatigue is being well prepared in advance of making a decision. Here are a few questions and suggestions.

Did You Do Enough Research on the Issue?

Sometimes when you're struggling to make a difficult decision, it's because you don't know enough about the issue. Have you taken the time to see the world through your customers' eyes? Have you done an appropriate amount of secondary research studying the issue? There will always be a degree of uncertainly, but the question to ask yourself is, do you feel you've learned as much as you need to, given the size of the risk and the costs of failure?

Did You Frame the Decision Well?

Another reason that people have difficulty coming to a decision is that they don't actually know what decision they're trying to make. For example, people can sit through a two-hour meeting unaware that they're on completely different pages regarding why they're there. One person leaves thinking that a decision was made. Another leaves thinking that all they had was a high-level brainstorming session. I recommend using a five-part decision brief to formalize the decision process. Here's a sample.

Decision Brief

1. *Description of decision.* We need to decide whether or not we feel it's a good idea to invest more resources into Project X.
2. *Decision timing.* This decision needs to be made by Friday, November 9, eight weeks from today, so that we can request additional funds at the executive team meeting.
3. *Decision responsibility.* As this is a critical decision, the entire team is responsible for aligning behind it and inputting into it before we move forward.
4. *Current decision stage.* Expand.
   I recommend choosing one of four stages: explore (initial discussions), expand (ensure that all options and thinking are on the table), decide (limit options to one worth pursuing), or define (pick the path forward).
5. *Intended outcome of this conversation.*
   a. Everyone has an opportunity to share her perspective on the issues.
   b. The team members are clear on one another's thinking regarding the pros and cons of different options.
   c. The team will be aligned regarding the time frame for making a final decision.
   d. If more research needs to be done, we will be clear as to what that research is.

Did Everyone Actually Align on the Decision?

Nothing undermines a decision more than to have head-nods of agreement, only to have people not support the decision once it's been made. Or worse, a few months later, they have no recollection that the decision was ever made. For clarification, I recommend formally recapping decisions with next steps and implications. Put it into writing—a quick e-mail, for instance.

Chapter 8 Summary

- ► The future never reveals itself in a set of clear implications and stepwise plans of action. People have to regularly stop, reflect on, and discuss the future to make sense of it.
- ► The two areas where individuals and teams struggle the most when it comes to getting clear and focused on the future are (1) failure to get thinking out on the table for all to see, understand, and discuss, and (2) failure to make choices and close doors.
- ► It's important to balance discussion and exploration with making choices. Too much of the former without the latter results in analysis paralysis. Too much of the latter without the former results in ill-thought-out decisions.
- ► When a team gets its thinking out on the table and makes a choice, this builds positive team energy.
- ► The biggest challenge to doing this kind of planning work usually isn't lack of skill or ability. It's setting aside the time to actually do it.

CHAPTER NINE

Predict Your Fail Points

One of the risks of leadership is thinking too positively when you plan and set expectations.

—ORI HADOMI, CEO, Mazor Robotics

The last three chapters were about choosing ideas to move forward with. This chapter is about finding holes in those ideas. The purpose is not to tear the ideas down, but to build them up so that they're as strong as they can be.

Fail points or pitfalls often seem obvious only in retrospect. When you're in the middle of a planning process and thinking at a conceptual level, pitfalls are easy to miss. You naturally step over things that might trip you up when you're "on the ground" executing. If you don't stop to intentionally identify and mitigate possible fail points, you will find them later, when they're bound to wreak more havoc. Classic examples of predictable fail points are underestimating the time and resources needed, overestimating how helpful internal and/or external partners will be, and not properly taking a competitor's actions into account.

You'll never identify all possible fail points. Trying to do so is a waste of time. But if you can identify the more obvious ones up front and get better at noticing others along the way more quickly, this will greatly increase your chances of success.

Cultivating the Capability to See Danger in Advance

Finding ways to get better at predicting fail points is the job of every leader. This next story, taken from the military, provides important insights for all types of leaders.

In July 2001, U.S. Navy Rear Admiral Tom Zelibor (now retired) was in command of the Carl Vinson Battle Group, consisting of eight ships and 7,000 people, which was being deployed to the Arabian Sea for Operation Southern Watch, monitoring the no-fly zone in southern Iraq. It was a routine deployment that battle groups had been doing for the past 11 years.

Zelibor had spent the previous year on a quite different task. He and his team had developed a technology tool called Knowledge Web (KWeb), part of the U.S. Navy's network-centric warfare push to go paperless and become more efficient and effective using Internet technologies for communication.

Since routine deployments have a lot of downtime, Zelibor thought the July 2001 trip would be an excellent opportunity to pilot-test KWeb. He removed all the old communication processes built around creating static documents and replaced them with network processes built around updating dynamic content via the web.

"There's nothing worse than a bored admiral at sea," Zelibor shared. "I figured, we'd try this new stuff with our small group of eight ships and see if we could make it work. If we had good results, we'd write up a white paper and see if we could get the Navy to change some things."

Zelibor's ships rounded the tip of southern India into the Arabian Sea on September 11, 2001. As the horrific events of the day unfolded, he saw the scope and importance of his mission change dramatically. His superior informed him that he was now running all at-sea operations in the Persian Gulf for what would become Operation Enduring Freedom. Zelibor would be in command of three carrier battle groups and many dozen coalition partners, in total 100 ships and 40,000 people.

"What my superior didn't know at the time was that I had restructured all of our old processes in order to test KWeb," recalled Zelibor. "I had a mild panic attack, followed by a few sleepless nights thinking about the implications of that decision. But at that point I didn't have any other options. We couldn't easily switch things back. KWeb was about to get one serious pilot test."

In the days after 9/11, Zelibor's first task was to put together 20 concepts of operations in preparation for different scenarios. For the first time ever, his team did all its planning via KWeb behind the Department of Defense's SIPRNet (Secret Internet Protocol Router Network). When superiors called him with questions, instead of sending documents, Zelibor would direct them to a URL that contained his plans. In fact, everything his team was doing was viewable via SIPRNet. If you had clearance, you could see it.

"It was a huge career risk," Zelibor recalled. "No one had worked this way before. No one had sent a superior to a web address when he asked for a report. My peers thought I was crazy. They thought I was opening myself up to a 10,000-mile-long screwdriver because everyone could see all my plans and would want to meddle in my business."

However, exactly the opposite happened.

Zelibor quickly saw two things as he pilot-tested KWeb. First, many of the small questions and calls from data-hungry superiors stopped because people could get all their answers online. Second, when someone did call, it wasn't for data, but rather to have an in-depth strategic conversation.

Most important, KWeb was allowing Zelibor and his team to spend more time on "what-if" conversations and less time generating PowerPoint documents for superiors, an affliction well known in corporations that now also pervaded the military. That shift in focus markedly improved their ability to see danger in advance.

"We'd always been proactive, but with KWeb in place, we were becoming more *predictive*," Zelibor explained. "Being proactive is planning in advance. Being predictive is anticipating nuanced issues during the planning phase. We were becoming more predictive because we had more time to focus on the big picture."

Zelibor has many examples of how his team's predictive capability helped avert threats out in the field, most of which he can't discuss. However, he did share one example that happened back home at the U.S. Naval Station in San Diego.

Following 9/11, the Navy had started surprise exercises to simulate real threats. As in actual battle conditions, Zelibor knew that the attacks were coming, but he didn't know when or where. Two days after arriving at port, he was having dinner with dignitaries at a seafood restaurant overlooking the San Diego Harbor. Not long after sitting down, out of the corner of his eye, he caught a glimpse of something that seemed out of place. He turned and saw a black Zodiac boat whipping along the seawall in the dark. It was heading toward his ship, carrying three men with guns, all dressed in black. Zelibor was fairly certain that the boat was going to try to penetrate his security as part of a simulated threat. As his tablemates listened in stunned disbelief, he called the force protection watch officer on his ship to alert him to the attack. Less than two minutes later, it was averted. Thankfully, it turned out to be only a naval exercise.

Zelibor feels that a main reason he spotted the boat that night was improved predictive capability. "Every time we come into port, we put a force protection plan together to protect against attacks. Usually, the exercise is a lot of document creation. This time, we spent much more energy on the what-if conversations. We spent more time asking ourselves, 'If we were the enemy, what would we try to do to us?' It's possible that I would have noticed the boat even if we hadn't had those conversations, but there's no doubt that they made me more aware, more on my toes, and better able to react."

At the end of our conversation, Zelibor reflected on predicting fail points. "You can go back and look at the 9/11 reports. The information was all there, the unusual behavior and many other signals. But that heightened awareness, and the predictive capability it creates, probably was not."

Predictive Capability Is Born in Conversation

With all the complex technology that Zelibor had installed on his ships, one of its biggest advantages had nothing to do with the technology per se. It freed up his team members' time so that they could have more strategic conversations to predict fail points.

Robust conversations are at the heart of predicting fail points, even in the most involved strategic planning techniques. Scenario planning, for example, is a structured process designed to make sense of many variables in complex situations.[1] Companies like Royal Dutch Shell use scenario planning to decide whether or not to invest hundreds of millions of dollars in a given project. If you walked into one of the company's scenario-planning sessions, you'd probably see matrices, systems diagrams, and spreadsheets. Upon completion of the session, however, most people in the room would tell you that, as important as the data were, the real value came from bringing to the surface and discussing intuitive assumptions about the forces that were at play.

Much smaller companies use simpler versions of scenario planning. Often these versions have a "back of the napkin" feel, but they can be equally useful.

Steven Kotok, president of *The Week*, a news and opinion magazine in the United States, has found a simple and effective way to bring assumptions to the surface and discuss them with his team. Owned by Dennis Publishing, the same U.K. company that launched *Maxim* magazine, *The Week* is one of the most successful newsweeklies currently in print. It is profitable and has increasing readership at a time when most of its competitors are losing both money and readers. In part, Kotok credits the magazine's success to its being able to quickly predict what will and won't work, and keeping things simple.

"New people who come to work for us are amazed at how little process we have," Kotok shared. "For the most part, we tend to see our lack of process as a good thing. Often, when you try to introduce too much process, you kill the common sense inherent in a good conversation."

As an example, when vetting new subscriber strategies, Kotok and his managers ask three basic questions to determine if something is worth using their resources to pursue. How easy or hard is it to execute? How likely is it to succeed? And how big is the revenue bump we can expect to get? If it doesn't pass the sniff test on any of these, it's relegated to the trash. In fact, conversations kill around 90 percent of new ideas before they ever see the light of day.

"You don't see spreadsheets in these meetings," Kotok explained. "It's just a group of managers who, over the years, have seen a bunch of ideas work and a lot of others fail. We have open conversations, getting thoughts and opinions out on the table and predicting what is worth our time and what isn't. It may be a simple process, but it's very efficient."

Seeing Fail Points *Inside* Your Team

The previous examples point primarily to external reasons why something might fail, such as market forces, competitive threats, or cost constraints. However, if you've ever taken a risk along with other people, like starting a business, tackling a tough project, or driving a big change, you know that often the biggest threats to success aren't external, they're internal. All sorts of dangers lurk inside a team that's trying to tackle a big problem. Predicting these internal dangers will also significantly increase the chances of success.

That's what Lee Kranefuss and his management team at iShares did.

Started inside of Barclays Global Investors (BGI) in 2000 to develop and sell exchange-traded funds (ETFs), iShares is widely regarded as one of the biggest retail investment success stories of the past decade. If you recall Jono Steinberg's story from Chapter 5, iShares is one of the companies that helped educate the market and pave the way for WisdomTree's own ETF success.

Over nine years, Kranefuss and his iShares team built what became the 800-pound gorilla in ETFs and the crown jewel in a $13 billion sale of BGI to BlackRock. By its tenth anniversary in 2010, iShares was managing more than $500 billion in investor assets—nearly half of all dollars invested in the entire ETF market.

From the outside, it would be easy to think that iShares succeeded on the power of a great idea alone, but that would be far from the truth. Internal friction on the iShares management team almost blew it up before it even got out of the starting block.

In the late 1990s, Kranefuss was the head of strategy at BGI. In that role, he had the task of finding new businesses for the company to pursue. One of those was ETFs, a small and relatively unknown investment vehicle at the time. His analysis of ETFs started as a debunking mission, trying to demonstrate why *not* to pursue the market.

However, he soon realized that he was looking at a diamond in the rough. The ETF product itself was very attractive. It had significant tax, transparency, and cost advantages over mutual funds. Its only weakness was its obscurity. He hypothesized that if people really understood ETFs and had easier access to them, they'd definitely invest in them. He further concluded that the primary reason people *didn't* know about them was that companies like Vanguard and Fidelity, which were in a position to market ETFs, had a vested interest in *not* doing so because they were afraid that ETFs would cannibalize their mutual fund business.

This led Kranefuss to his critical insight. If BGI were willing to go big enough from the beginning, simultaneously educating the market and launching a large platform of funds, it could build and eventually dominate the ETF market. It was a huge bet. Kranefuss concluded that the company would have to reach $100 billion in assets under management just to break even. It would take a Herculean effort. He sold the idea to then BGI CEO Pattie Dunn. She got on board, giving him three years to get it to profitability.

A year later, in March 2000, Kranefuss had a top-notch team in place working at breakneck speed in order to launch 35 new funds by year-end, starting in May, an unheard-of number in the investment fund world.

"I had serious doubts that we were going to make the May deadline," recalls J. Parsons, head of sales and employee 2. "If we did, it was going to be by working 'round the clock. And even then it was going to be really close. We started scheduling meetings in 5- to 10-minute increments because 15 minutes was just too long. Every second counted."

It was at this pivotal point that Kranefuss suddenly pulled everyone offsite for three days to talk about how they were working together.

"I thought he was nuts. The whole team did," recalls Mike Latham, COO at the time and now chairman of iShares. "Here we are, firing on all cylinders just to get ourselves on the map, and he wants to put on the brakes for some navel-gazing. It was one of the few times I questioned his judgment."

But Kranefuss put his foot down, and they held the offsite. The primary focus was to get challenges and issues out on the table. It wasn't long before the other team members saw what Kranefuss had seen. There were little fissures in their relationships—little differences that, under stress, were starting to cause cracks. With the help of an outside facilitator, the team members gave direct feedback to each other.

"Twelve years later, I still carry the notes that I received at that offsite," Parsons shared. "It made a huge impact on me. I'm a big guy with a strong personality. What I didn't realize until then was that people were experiencing me as aggressive, gruff, and angry toward them. That might work for a little while, but it wouldn't work well for very long. I realized I had to change some things. Everyone had his own version of an insight like that."

Latham shared the operational implications for the team. "Nothing big had fallen through the cracks at that point, but after those conversations, we realized that things were about to. We were pushing so hard that we weren't taking the time to discuss issues together. Furthermore, the pace wasn't going to slow down in May; it was only going to get faster and more complex. If we hadn't figured out how to become a higher-performing team at that point, we very well might have imploded—and who knows what iShares would be today."

IDEAS AND TOOLS FOR ACTION

Mike Latham's comment about putting on the brakes for the offsite highlights an important fact about predicting fail points—you have to *stop* to do it. The difficulty is, it often doesn't feel natural to stop when you are pushing forward on something. Once you've taken so much time and energy to see the future strategically and plot out a path to get there, the last thing you want to think about is how you might fail. So most people don't do it. However, if you get into the habit of knowing that this kind of predicting is important and expecting to do it on a regular basis, it becomes much easier.

Use Specific Questions for Fail-Point Brainstorming

Chapter 8 introduced the idea of asking strategic questions by giving the four that Sam Palmisano used at IBM. Key questions are also important to guide thinking around fail points. Of those that I've collected over the years, I've found that the five given here are the most useful. For a given discussion, pick one or two questions that are germane to the issues that you're most concerned about.

▶ *On a scale of 1 to 10, what is my personal level of commitment to this effort and why?* (This uncovers a common fail point: lack of commitment.)

▶ *If in 12 months we deem this effort a total failure, what will have caused it?* (This uncovers issues that the team members are already thinking could bring them down, but that they aren't discussing together.)

▶ *If in 12 months we haven't made the progress we had hoped to make, what will have caused it?* (This uncovers issues that the team members are already thinking could slow them down, but that they aren't discussing together.)

▶ *Who is going to be actively working against us in our efforts to succeed? And what will they try to do?* (This broad question gets the team members thinking about internal and external forces that may get in their way.)

▶ *If we were our competitors, how would we try to beat us?*
(This puts you in the shoes of your competitors to see what
weaknesses they may try to exploit.)

I recommend that you do fail-point brainstorming in a separate
meeting from one in which you are *setting* strategy. It's difficult to
generate ideas, get excited about them, and then have to shoot
holes in them on the same day.

It's also important that you create a safe space within which to
have this conversation. If the whole group or some subset is enthu-
siastic about the ideas you're shooting holes in, defensiveness can
arise. Frame the conversation up front as an exercise to strengthen
the idea by welcoming all thoughts and concerns.

Map Brainstormed Fail Points

Once you've generated a helpful list of possible fail points (usually
10 to 20), map them against two variables, degree of control and
degree of concern, using the 2 × 2 matrix in Figure 9.1.

Degree of control refers to how much influence the team has
over a given fail point. Degree of concern refers to how worried the
team is about that particular fail point. The two biggest factors that
go into degree of concern are the likelihood of occurrence and the
strategic impact of the fail point.

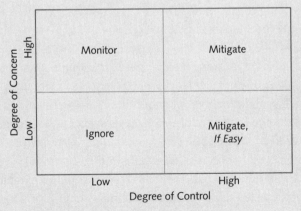

FIGURE 9.1   HOW MIGHT WE FAIL?

To see what it looks like in action, let's pretend that three people—Mark, Bob, and Brenda—are considering opening a cookie store on Main Street in their hometown. They answer the question, "If in 12 months we haven't made the progress we had hoped to make, what will have caused it?" And they brainstorm the following list of possible fail points:

- ► Underestimate timing
- ► Underestimate complexity
- ► Partners get into argument
- ► Cost of goods goes up
- ► Regulatory risk
- ► Current competitors' actions
- ► New competitors' actions
- ► Finding employees
- ► Relationships with suppliers and partners
- ► Customer preference changes
- ► Securing financing

They map them on the matrix as shown in Figure 9.2:

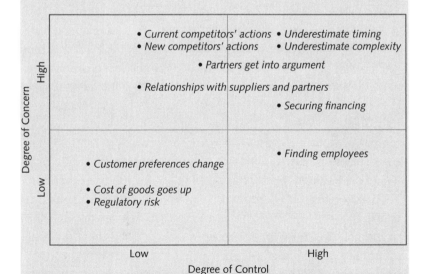

FIGURE 9.2   MAPPING POSSIBLE FAIL POINTS FOR A NEW VENTURE

Following the mapping, the three partners debrief the exercise. The first thing they discuss is how helpful it is to see their big concerns in one place. While making a list is useful, mapping the list clarifies the relative importance of each. Then their discussion of specific fail points brings the whole picture into clearer view.

It was Brenda who listed "underestimate timing" and "underestimate complexity." As a former pharmaceutical IT director, she is well aware of how projects can go off the rails. With less project management experience, Mark and Bob hadn't been obsessing about these issues as much. But as Brenda walks them through her thinking, Mark and Bob realize there is a level of complexity on a few issues that they hadn't considered. All three agree that it belongs in the top right of the matrix.

Conversely, as a financial analyst, Bob is used to focusing on high-level market risks and what's happening on the world stage from an economic perspective. He suggested the ideas that cost of goods might rise and regulatory risk as things that could affect profitability. However, after a brief discussion, the group agrees that it can ignore these issues, as they have a low likelihood of having a significant impact on them. If they should become a problem, there's little the partners can do about them.

Mark was most worried about the competition and added current and new competitors' actions to the brainstorm list. Initially, the group had put both of these squarely in the top left box because, while they were concerned about competitors, they figured that they didn't have much control over them. However, as they discuss the topic further, they agree that they might be considering the issue too narrowly. While it's true that they can't actually control what competitors do, they can protect against competitors' actions. Bob mentions that his daughter has a gluten allergy and can never find good gluten-free baked goods. If they pick a particular niche in the cookie market, like gluten-free, maybe they can get out in front of the competition with a focused message. They therefore end up pushing competitors' actions further into their realm of control because they feel they can mitigate them to some degree through market positioning.

Plan to Mitigate and Monitor

Once you have identified, mapped, and discussed fail points, you want to come up with a plan to address them. Continuing with the previous example, Mark, Bob, and Brenda make the following mitigation plans.

Since underestimating timing and complexity and securing financing are the biggest concerns, the group agrees that a stronger business plan is a good idea. Brenda takes the lead and will tap a friend who has opened a retail store before to help identify specific thoughts and ideas.

The possibility that the partners might get into an argument that causes a rift is something else that they want to ensure doesn't happen. They agree to have monthly partner meetings to "shoot straight" with one another about issues and concerns.

To create a clearer niche and protect against competitive threats in the future, Bob agrees to do more research on the gluten-free market to understand the viability of a store with that focus. Also, to stay abreast of what competitors are doing, the partners agree to visit competitive stores regularly to understand their offerings.

None of these mitigation strategies is hard. This cookie store example shows the "right-under-your-nose" nature of many fail points. Will Mark, Bob, and Brenda find and address all of the possible fail points? No way. But will they create a level of awareness that helps them address some and stay aware of others as they arise? You bet. It's the same for large companies. The hardest part of predicting fail points is exercising the muscle to see them in the first place.

Chapter 9 Summary

▶ You'll never identify all the possible fail points in a given endeavor. Trying to do so is a waste of time. But identifying some of the more obvious ones up front and getting quicker at noticing others along the way greatly increase your chances of success.

▶ The time and energy put into predicting fail points will vary depending on the perceived cost of failure. A company deciding to spend $100 million on a five-year project will take more time and energy to do its predictions than a company that is executing hundreds of small projects every year.

▶ Whether it's a brief or an involved process, predictive capability doesn't come from fancy technology or techniques, but rather from honest, in-depth conversations. The more often you're able to consider the what-ifs of the situations you're facing, the better you get at predicting fail points.

▶ While it's common to look for fail points externally in things like market forces, competitive threats, and cost constraints, some of the more insidious ones are internal, like friction on a team.

▶ Brainstorming and mapping fail points is the best way for a team to get aligned on the issues its members all see. This provides the requisite foundation for mitigation planning.

PART FOUR

ACT FAST, LEARN FAST

Start Before You Know Where to Start

When one has finished building one's house, one suddenly realizes that in the process one has learned something that one really needed to know in the worst way—before one began.

—FRIEDRICH NIETZSCHE

There's a moment, after you've done all your planning and you're standing on the edge of a risk, debating whether or not to jump in, when you realize that logical analysis has taken you as far as it can and it's never going to convince you to take that final step. Too much still feels uncertain. You realize that if you're going to take that final step, it's going to have to be a leap of faith.

I call this the *kinetic moment*. It's the moment when you see the potential in something and decide to make a move, even though you still have doubts. Kinetic moments are often filled with heart palpitations, sweaty palms, and butterflies. They're characterized by an indescribable mixture of excitement, tension, terror, and relief.

We reach kinetic moments for one reason: *not risking* seems scarier than risking. We rarely love the thought of taking action in these moments, but we hate the thought of not taking action. So we act.

An example is the musician who feels stage fright but takes the stage anyway because he can't imagine not playing his music for others. Or an average, usually quiet citizen who speaks up because not saying something feels too irresponsible. Or an entrepreneur who is hesitant to invest in a new idea, but who jumps in because not taking her shot is unimaginable.

Once you jump in, you often learn an important lesson: your initial fears were largely unfounded. Things weren't as difficult as you thought they would be. You found support where you least expected it. And you were more capable than you realized.

You just had to start moving in order to understand this.

The Art of Starting

If you don't start somewhere, you'll never get anywhere. I'm always amazed at how this little truism trips people up time and time again. I include myself. I'll have an idea, think about it, plan for it, and then sit on it for a while, waiting for the timing to be better before getting started. But better timing never comes. The idea keeps eating at me. I think about it some more, and finally I just jump in. Within days, I always have the same thought: worrying about starting was much more painful than doing it.

As a case in point, when I was writing this book, I wasn't sure how to approach several chapters and what exactly I wanted to say. I sat down to think about them. Then I thought some more. Then I thought even more. Weeks passed. Finally, out of desperation, I started writing. To my surprise, what came out on the page looked completely different from what I had been thinking about for so long. There was something about writing that reoriented me and made me realize what the chapter really needed to say. Once the chapter was complete, I vowed never to get myself into that spot again. Then, two chapters later—you guessed it, stuck again.

For me, the good news was that each bout of paralysis got shorter as I found little things I could do to get me into action faster. I could talk ideas into a recorder first, or just start writing a stream of consciousness, or have others interview me before I wrote. Through the process, I gained a deeper appreciation that starting is an art, and that I had to (and *have to*) keep experimenting with ways to start in order to get better at it.

Physics is instructive in the art of starting. Two laws in particular, inertia and momentum, are helpful reminders.

Inertia is the resistance of a body to changes in its state of motion. The only way a body goes from rest to motion, or from motion to rest, is through the addition of an outside force. That means that while it takes a force to put something in motion, it's the exact opposite once something is already in motion—it takes a force to stop it.

Momentum is mass multiplied by velocity. Once a body is in motion, every nudge forward is additive and builds steam. The more momentum something has, the harder it becomes to stop. The implications of inertia and momentum for risk taking are profound. When you start moving, physics is your friend. When you don't move, it's your worst enemy.

Often, the amount of force needed to start something isn't that big. It can be a single conversation, document, or meeting. It doesn't have to solve every problem. In fact, it doesn't even have to be the right move. It just has to get things in motion. It just has to lead to another action. And then another. It's easy to get so fixated on a big end goal that you discount the small efforts needed to start a process. You think they'll barely make a dent in what you're trying to do. However, it's only through repeated small efforts that you ever make progress.

What Improv Theater Can Teach Us About Risk Taking

A few years ago, while I was attending an improvisational comedy workshop, I got a good reminder of the power of small efforts and starting before you know where to start.

I had lost a bet with a friend and, against my wishes, was accompanying her to the workshop as payment. I say against my wishes because to me, improv is the ultimate in anxiety-producing situations. You're performing before an audience with no preparation, trying to get a laugh. And you're most certainly about to make a fool of yourself.

On stage that night, all my fears were realized. As the scene turned to me, I panicked and went blank. I felt my face flush. I didn't know what to do next. Out of desperation, I blurted out some nonsense about wanting to play baseball. The comment was utterly ridiculous, because at that point we were supposedly on a flight from New York to Miami.

In true improv fashion, another actor chimed in without missing a beat, "That's a great suggestion, Doug. Anyone can play baseball outside. But it takes real skill to play it on an airplane between the passengers and the seats. Thankfully, I have a bag of bats, balls, and gloves in the overhead bin!"

For the next two minutes, we played a full inning of imaginary baseball 35,000 feet above the Atlantic. It was very funny.

As I reflected on the experience later, I saw that my initial anxiety was born from a fear that I would somehow screw up. And yet there I was, screwing up, wanting to play baseball on an airplane, and yet the scene worked. Doing the "right" thing in that moment was much less important than merely doing *something*. My inane comment gave us all what we needed—motion.

I'm still in touch with my teacher from that workshop, Scotty Watson, a comedian and an alum of the renowned Second City comedy troupe. In addition to his work on stage, Watson also runs corporate improv workshops designed to enhance creativity and leadership effectiveness. A big part of the hurdle he helps leaders and teams overcome is starting before they know where to start.

"Starting is everything," Watson believes. "If you don't start, nothing happens. You can apply that to anything in life. Without starting, nothing happens in your scene, nothing happens in your business, nothing happens in your relationships—the list goes on. Even starting in the wrong direction is better than not starting at all because at least something is happening. I always tell my students and clients, 'Do something. Do anything. Just start!'"

Watson believes that starting in the wrong direction not only is a good alternative to doing nothing, but can often be the *best* way to start something because it wakes people up, creates tension, and causes reactions, much like my baseball comment. As Watson describes it, "No one falls asleep when someone's screwing up."

One of the funniest scenes he can remember involved an industry veteran, Adrian Truss, mistakenly breaking the number one rule of improv by saying "no" to another actor's suggestion—usually a kiss of death because it kills a scene's flow.

"Watching Truss screw up and then dig himself out of that hole was surprising, interesting, and hilarious, but most of all, it was memorable," recalls Watson. "The proof is the fact that I'm telling you about it right now. If everything had gone according to plan, I would have forgotten about that scene years ago."

Bad starts with a good recovery have sticking power and story value.

Watson adds that you don't have to do anything wild or off the wall to start something. He draws an important distinction between "big C" creativity and "little c" creativity. "Big C" creativity is a game-changing new idea. "Little c" creativity is a small step that changes something right under your nose.

"In improv and in business, 99.9 percent of all creativity is 'little c' creativity," Watson explained. "That's where true innovation comes from. It's small changes on top of small changes. It's continuous little risks. And even 'big C' creativity is usually just a lot of 'little c' creativity added up. No one just drops an idea for the next iPad in a suggestion box. It takes a lot of little starts."

To help clients and students get over the fear of starting, Watson reminds them of three cardinal principles developed by improv great Elaine May. He feels they apply to risk taking on stage, in business, or anywhere in life:

1. *Make active and positive choices.* When you do things in good faith and to the best of your abilities, no matter what happens, good will come from it.

2. *Support the reality around you.* When you start where you
   are, accepting the world around you just as it is, you gain
   power.
3. *Don't worry about making mistakes, just fix them.* When you
   make a mistake, take responsibility for it, fix it, and keep moving. Often this leads to the most interesting outcomes.

In parting, Watson shared one of the best insights of our
conversation. It's a line he tells himself all the time. "You have
everything you need in order to be successful in the present moment. The only time you get into trouble is when you
doubt that fact. Start where you are, with what you have, and
everything works itself out."

That's a great thought to keep in mind when you're jumping into the unknown.

Getting a Medical Device Through the FDA

At some time or another, we all have to jump into the
unknown. We're put in a position where, with little or no help
from others, we have to figure out how to do something that's
completely new to us. It's rarely as complex as getting FDA
clearance to sell a surgically implanted spinal device. But that's
exactly what the 28-year-old biomedical engineer Jennifer
Palinchik did.

Palinchik's boss at a small engineering firm outside of
Cleveland asked her to try to get FDA 510(k) clearance for one
of a client's medical devices. A complicated multistep undertaking, the 510(k) process is something that manufacturers
often hire specialized regulatory consulting firms to handle.
In this case, the client was small and didn't have a huge budget, and Palinchik's boss figured that if they could do it, the
client would be appreciative and her firm would gain a new
product offering.

"I had no idea where to start," Palinchik recalled. "In fact,
I thought it was a little crazy for me to even try to do it. First,
there are usually whole departments that handle documentation like this. Second, I knew how to design things, but
nothing about navigating the regulation process. To me, the

FDA was a big government agency filled with red tape that I wasn't interested in learning about. The whole thing seemed really daunting."

But with encouragement from her boss, she just jumped in anyway. Her first step was to spend several days searching through the FDA website just to understand what she'd gotten herself into. Those first few days did little to alleviate her concerns about red tape, as she saw that the FDA website was filled with so much guidance that it felt unclear and sometimes conflicting to a newcomer. Nonetheless, she mapped out a plan and pushed forward.

A key part of the process was doing predicate device research, or identifying similar medical devices that had already received clearance for sale and use. Demonstrating similarity to predicate devices could significantly reduce submission and clearance times and thus time to market for her client. Palinchik thought this was great news, as it would make her job easier. Then she started searching through the FDA's Product Classification Database.

"Let's just say that it wasn't like doing a simple Google search," Palinchik explained. "Not only was I looking for devices, but I was simultaneously learning the arcane FDA classification system, which was not at all intuitive to me at the time."

Finally, after a few weeks, Palinchik had chosen her predicate devices and had completed the application documents. Having heard horror stories about applications getting kicked back over and over for further information, she reviewed her application thoroughly to make sure she was putting her best foot forward. Still, since this was her first try, she was sure she'd have to do significant reworking a few months down the road.

To her surprise, however, the FDA came back with a relatively minor request for further information. She provided the information and got the clearance. All told, the process took just under a year, which was within the normal 9- to 12-month range for most applications.

"My anxiety at the beginning of the processes was worse than the process itself," Palinchik reflected. "A few parts were challenging, but overall it wasn't that difficult. In retrospect, it was probably one of the most rewarding experiences in my life. In less than a year, I figured out how to navigate the FDA approval process and got a spinal device cleared to sell and use in the United States."

Palinchik's story doesn't end there. A year later, her company was bought by Matt Hlavin at Thogus, the custom injection molder introduced in Chapter 7. It wasn't until months after Palinchik came on board at Thogus that Hlavin learned that she had experience with the FDA 510(k) process. He quickly saw it as an important piece of a new service: offering to help small medical manufacturers go to market. It was a business that he wanted Palinchik to lead and grow.

Before she knew it, Palinchik was staring at another big challenge.

"I felt anxiety all over again, a new, bigger anxiety," Palinchik recalled. "I had done one submission, and now Matt wanted me to roll them into a service offering and go to market with a beginning-to-end product. At first I thought, 'Am I ready for this?' But then I thought back to what I'd accomplished over the last couple of years and realized that I hadn't been ready for that, either. And yet I did it. You're never really ready to take on a new challenge. You just do it."

Palinchik and her team are now working on getting their fifth device approved by the FDA, and Thogus's medical device business is booming.

Starting a New Career from Scratch

Sometimes starting something new can be incremental. Sometimes, as in Bruce Schoenberg's case, it's a big leap of faith.

In 1996, after 20 years in the trade-show business and more than 2,000 days on the road, Schoenberg was looking for a change of pace. He had just gotten married, and he wanted to do something closer to home. An entrepreneur at heart, he began exploring business ideas. His wife, Marti, a massage therapist, suggested that they look into the possibility of opening a spa.

"At the time, I knew nothing about spas. I had never even been to one," Schoenberg admitted. "All I knew was that there were already a ton of spas in New York City, and, as in any capital-intensive business, there were probably a thousand ways to lose your shirt. It didn't seem like an attractive opportunity to me."

However, Marti saw the opportunity for a high-quality spa that wasn't off-the-charts expensive—a niche that she felt was underserved. Powered by Marti's suggestion, Schoenberg threw himself into researching the spa business for six months. In that time, he personally visited more than 50 spas to better understand price points, services, and experiences. At the end of his research, he and Marti came to the conclusion that her initial gut sense was right. The high-end, yet affordable market was a perfect target. He spent months writing a business plan and exploring financing options before making the decision to jump in.

"That final decision was scary," Schoenberg remembers. "No matter how much research I did, I was still taking a leap of faith. There were so many unknowns that could have brought us down. I'd done a lot of focus groups, but I knew that focus groups weren't necessarily indicative of real consumer behavior because market conditions can turn on a dime. I was second- and third-guessing myself, but we just decided to jump in and trust that we could handle any adversity that came up."

In November 1998, sitting behind his grandmother's card table as a makeshift front desk (because the desk he'd ordered was a month late showing up), Schoenberg welcomed his first customers to Oasis Day Spa in Manhattan's Union Square. That's when his real education began.

"That first year was a steep learning curve," Schoenberg explained. "I'd never been in retail before, and I soon realized that selling directly to consumers is a much different game from selling to businesses. It's a more emotion-based sell. I wasted money on direct mail that had the wrong messaging. I bought advertising in the wrong publications. I didn't understand the power of coupons, discounts, and giveaways to drive consumer behavior. And I didn't stock products quickly enough, losing significant revenue in the process."

As challenging as these lessons were, Schoenberg believes he learned them the only way he could have. "In retrospect, jumping in was the only way for me to truly appreciate what it would take to succeed in retail. People had warned me about some of these things in advance, but I still had to make the mistakes myself. It's like cooking; just because you have the recipe in front of you doesn't mean that you're going to nail it the first time you make it. It takes practice."

Schoenberg practiced for 18 months, and by the end of 1999, Oasis Day Spa was in the black and growing steadily.

Fourteen years later, with three locations in the New York metropolitan area, Oasis Day Spa is a certified success story. It's been named to *New York* magazine's "Best of New York" list twice, and it has won the coveted *DaySpa* magazine Diamond Award. It's successfully weathered its fair share of bumps along the way, including a fire in one of its locations in 2006 and the 2008 recession, which put many of its competitors out of business.

Schoenberg has a good business head, which has gone a long way toward ensuring Oasis's success. But he's also the first to admit that most of what's made Oasis successful he's learned along the way.

"There are so many things in business that you just can't predict, or that you underestimate," Schoenberg said. "You can't figure them all out in advance. If you try to, you'll paralyze yourself. We brought a basic philosophy to Oasis: provide great spa services and keep our eye on the bottom line. All the other critical details had to be learned on the road."

IDEAS AND TOOLS FOR ACTION

No matter what you do, starting before you know where to start will always feel somewhat disorienting. You're doing things you've never done before. The exercises that follow can help you decrease your anxiety enough to begin to put inertia and momentum on your side.

Identify the First Three Steps

At the outset of any significant risk, you're in a Catch-22. You don't feel you can get started until you know what you need to do. However, you won't know what you need to do until you get started. One way to get past this dilemma is to put pen to paper and write down the first three steps you'd take to get started. Crystalizing your ideas around initial steps breaks down the size of the risk and clearly delineates a path for progress where one didn't exist before. It works for small risks, big risks, or anywhere you feel stuck.

The quality of the steps you choose is less important than the process of choosing them. Choosing three directionally "good" steps now is better than choosing three "perfect" steps later because it builds momentum.

Following are examples from clients to give you an idea of what this process looks like. Getting your thoughts down on paper is an important part of the process.

Making a Difficult Management Decision

Situation
When taking over a new role, a vice president at a software firm inherited what she felt was a team of "B+" players. She wanted to clean house immediately, but she was afraid that doing so might damage client relationships, send fear through her organization, and reflect poorly on her because some of her B+ players were politically connected to executives above her. The prospect of tip-toeing through this minefield felt daunting.

First Three Steps (in the VP's Voice)
1. *Create a clear profile of each team member.* Having a more nuanced, fact-based understanding of each team member will help me form my own opinions and limit the risk of my being influenced by hearsay.
2. *Create a clear profile of each client.* Knowing the specific state of each client relationship will clarify where true gaps and opportunities lie.

3. *Set a specific strategic task for team members.* Giving each team member an opportunity to step up to new challenges will provide a future-focused view of the team members' capabilities.

Outcome

These first three steps helped the vice president develop conviction concerning ideas that had been vague. She realized that two of the team members were really A players who had slipped into B+ habits. Two of them were closer to B material, and she was clearer now on why they had to go. The fifth was B+, but he had enough redeeming qualities that she wanted to keep him. She noticed that much of her anxiety decreased as she went through these first three steps.

Pursuing a Large Business Opportunity

Situation

A junior partner at a small consulting firm wanted to pursue a new project that was bigger than anything the firm had done before. While it was exciting, he would be venturing into uncharted waters, and he didn't have a clear path to success. In moving forward, he wanted to put himself in the best position to win and ensure that he wasn't wasting his own and other people's time if it was a bad idea from the start.

First Three Steps (in the Partner's Voice)

1. *Create a one-page deal synopsis and get buy-in from other partners.* Having clear descriptions of the pros and cons of the deal and why I think we can and should pursue it will help others see the deal the same way I'm seeing it.
2. *Develop a detailed description of the client's needs and objectives.* Ensuring that I understand the client's goals will help focus my thinking on what will be required in the pursuit and delivery of the project.
3. *Create the high-level work plan required to meet the client's needs and objectives.* Defining a framework for delivering this project will help me see it in manageable parts and decrease my anxiety about its size.

Outcome

These first three steps gave him and his partners the confidence that their firm could handle a client this size. They also allowed him to be more assertive and proactive in the initial client meeting. Ultimately, he ended up losing this specific piece of business, but he won another contract of comparable size 12 months later, largely because of the confidence the first pursuit gave him.

Ask Yourself, What's the Worst That Could Happen?

If you've done your planning and you think the risk is a good idea, but you still find it tough to move forward, the following exercise will be useful. It helps you distinguish between what's truly likely to happen and what you might be overthinking or catastrophizing about. Brainstorm the answers to two questions. Allow time to really think about them and get others' input.

> ► What is the worst that could happen if we move forward?
> ► What is the likelihood of each of those things happening?

Often the conversation around these questions will help you see two things. First, the worst that could happen, while not desirable, usually isn't as catastrophic as it seems in your mind. Just airing your biggest fears tends to diminish how catastrophic they feel. Second, the likelihood of the worst-case scenario happening is often much less than it seems. Because this scenario is so undesirable, it tends to occupy a larger share of your mind than it deserves. Through doing this exercise, you find that the more likely challenges are things that you'll be able to handle.

Read About Successful Risk Takers (or Go Talk to Them)

There's something reassuring about knowing that before starting Microsoft, Bill Gates and Paul Allen tried to build a company called Traf-O-Data that failed—and that the lessons they learned from that attempt were critical to their later success. Or that Walt Disney was once turned down for a job as a newspaper cartoonist because he "lacked imagination." Or that one of Masaru Ibuka and Akio Morita's first products at Sony was a rice cooker that never sold well because it burned the rice. When we hear, and, more important, understand, the trials, tribulations, and eventual success of others, it makes it easier for us to get started on our own.

Chapter 10 Summary

- ▶ The *kinetic moment* is the moment when you decide to take a risk even though you still have doubts. Logic alone can never compel you beyond the kinetic moment. Reaching it takes a leap of faith—starting before you know exactly where to start.
- ▶ All of us reach paralysis points in starting something difficult. It's helpful to remember that the force needed to start something is usually smaller than we realize. It can be a single conversation, document, or meeting.
- ▶ Improvisational theater teaches us that if we start where we are, with what we have, and with good intentions, things have a way of working out in the end.
- ▶ Even the most daunting tasks, like getting a spinal device approved by the FDA or changing careers in midlife, are accomplished by taking one step at a time and learning as you go.
- ▶ Clarifying the first three steps needed to start something decreases fear and increases the propensity for action.

CHAPTER ELEVEN

Fail Early, Often, and Smart

Perfectionism is the enemy of creation.

—JOHN UPDIKE, American writer

One of the questions I ask clients who are about to take a risk is: "What are your thoughts on failure?" The question usually garners a nervous chuckle, followed by a response along the lines of: "I don't like it, and I try to avoid it at all costs.

Wanting to ease my clients' anxiety, I ask them to reflect on a productive failure—a misstep or difficult situation that turned out to be surprisingly beneficial. Within 30 seconds, most people can usually think of at least one. It's often a compelling story of a struggle that led to personal development, the development of the person's business, or both. When I ask whether, given the choice, they'd forgo that failure, most people say they wouldn't. Their reasoning is that while it may have been uncomfortable, the failure was pivotal in helping them succeed in the long run. Most of them also say that the upside of their failure far outweighed the downside.

Chapter 9 pointed out ways to predict fail points so that you could mitigate as much risk as possible up front. This chapter is about dealing with the risks and fail points that you didn't predict, embracing them as a necessary part of risk taking.

Failure is essential to progress. On the one hand, we know that, but on the other hand, it's easy to forget. Failure helps us uncover new learning, ideas, and approaches that we find only by taking a few wrong turns. To avoid failure is to avoid creativity and innovation because anything new rarely works on the first try. In any endeavor, failing early, often, and intelligently is at the root of success.

Reframing Failure

When I was 24 years old, I fell into a position as the business development director at a small New York advertising agency. I had met the agency owner, Bill Markel, two weeks earlier at an advertising awards show. I happened to be attending the event with a friend for the free food and drinks. As we left, Bill was standing next to me in the coat check line, holding an award he'd just won. I congratulated him, we struck up a conversation, and he mentioned that he was looking to hire someone in business development. It sounded like a great opportunity, so I threw my hat in the ring. Two weeks later, I had the job. At the time, I knew nothing about the ad industry. I was just an ambitious guy who felt that I could tackle anything with enough elbow grease. Apparently, Bill thought so too.

I had no idea how tough the job would be.

Selling ad agency services is complex. You're selling ideas, relationships, and the promise of something that people can't touch—all for a large price tag. It's hard enough when you have experience and know what you're doing. It's next to impossible when you have a baby face and an empty Rolodex.

For the first few months, I could barely find a potential client to talk to, let alone anyone to sell something to. I was quickly realizing that I'd bitten off more than I could chew. I was also questioning Bill's judgment in having hired me in the first place. At least *I* could plead ignorance. But this guy had been in the business for years and should've known better than to put someone my age in this position. How in the world did he think that a young guy with no experience was going to waltz into the C-suites of major corporations and be taken seriously?

Every Thursday, Bill and I would review my deal pipeline. On one occasion, three months into my tenure, I was feeling particularly dejected. We were having one of those dreadful meetings that all salespeople hate—you have nothing going on and nothing to say, but you have to say something, so you just start talking.

I babbled about different deals, trying to justify my lack of progress. All the while, I was getting sick of my own voice. If I had been sitting across from myself, I'd have told me to stop talking. I was desperately hoping Bill would do just that. No such relief. Bill just let me keep going.

Finally, exasperated and out of justifications, I stopped and said, "Bill, I don't know what I'm doing here. I think this job was a mistake for me. I don't have enough experience to do it well, and I feel like I'm failing."

A smirk came across Bill's face. I remember thinking that I wasn't in the mood for whatever "words of wisdom" he was about to share. I never appreciated a pep talk of platitudes when I was frustrated about something. But his comment was short, sweet, and exactly what I needed to hear.

"I think you've got it backwards," he said.

"What do you mean?" I asked.

"You need to fail *more*."

He went on to make the point that my problem wasn't that I was failing. It was that I wasn't failing *enough*. I'd take a few good swings at something, but then stop if I hadn't gotten a hit. I wasn't striking out enough.

For the next month, he asked me to stop bringing my sales pipeline to our weekly meetings. Instead, he wanted me to bring my strikeouts. He wanted to hear about every attempt that didn't work out. The more the better. All of a sudden, our meetings had more levity. I felt freer to try new things.

A month later, Bill pushed me further. In my attempt to make more mistakes, I'd been pursuing a big fish—Mattel. I found out that the company would be presenting at an ad industry conference in New Orleans, and I suggested to Bill that if we could get a meeting set up in advance, we should go down and meet with them.

"I agree," Bill replied. "But you can handle this one alone. And I think you should go even if you can't get the meeting set up in advance. Just make the meeting happen once you get there."

Two weeks later, against my better judgment, I was on a plane alone to New Orleans. I didn't have a meeting set up with Mattel, and I had no game plan beyond just trying to find someone from the company to talk to. Bill's parting words were still ringing in my ears, "Just go down there and swing the bat."

When I got there, I felt like a teenager at his parents' cocktail party. I had no idea whom to talk to or what to talk to them about. I had one awkward conversation after another. It started to become a little game, just trying to see how many conversations I could scare up. At the end of the second day, I finally found an opportunity to talk to a VP from Mattel as she was leaving the conference. It wasn't the best timing, but better late than never.

I introduced myself, told her that I appreciated her presentation, and that we'd learned a few things working with M&M'S (one of our current clients) that I'd love to share with her. She gave me her business card and told me to give her a call. The whole thing lasted less than a minute. At the time, I was pretty sure she was just brushing me off. But I'd done what I was there to do, swing the bat.

When I got back to New York, I gave her a call and left a message. To my surprise, she returned the call a few hours later, and we had a good conversation. Several more conversations followed, and I got us into a pitch for a new Mattel/Intel joint venture. Six months later, after beating out two other agencies, we were awarded a half-million-dollar piece of business. It was my first significant sale, and it felt great.

What Bill knew in those early months, but I didn't appreciate until years later, was that all those initial failures were strengthening me. Telling me to "fail more" was his way of telling me to keep training—and to stop worrying about winning the race. By the time he sent me to New Orleans, he knew I was ready. He knew I'd had enough disastrous meetings and phone calls to know what worked and what didn't.

The trip was his attempt to get me to see it. I may have chatted with the Mattel VP for only 45 seconds that day, but there were four months of failure behind that conversation—and that's what made it a success.

I'm thankful to Bill for that lesson all those years ago. Looking back, I realize that he was doing more than giving me a paternal shot in the arm and saying, "Hey, don't worry about it. Everyone fails. You'll get them next time." He was helping me reframe failure. He wanted me to see failure as a sign of progress, not of weakness or incompetence.

Early Failures That Launched a Printing Business

Everyone who's ever succeeded has a story similar to mine. They try something over and over, seemingly not making progress, rethink their assumptions, recalibrate, and then finally, "pop"—a few battle scars later, the idea works. That also happened to Richard Moross at moo.com.

Self-described design nerd Moross founded moo.com in 2006 to give customers the opportunity to create business cards that stand out and communicate their unique identity. Today MOO has throngs of loyal customers evangelizing its products in more than 200 countries. It's carved out a lucrative niche in the printing market for people who want customized, creative, high-end products.

In 2004, with the same mission, Moross founded a predecessor to MOO, Pleasure Cards, which failed miserably. The misfires at Pleasure Cards and the eventual global success of MOO provide an instructive example of why failure is unavoidable and often becomes the catalyst for subsequent success.

A former strategist at the world's largest independent design company, Imagination, Moross knew good and bad design. In founding Pleasure Cards, he wanted to share his design point of view with the world. Moross first envisioned the company as more of a fashion label than a platform for people to create their own identities. The business was more about Moross's ideas and what he felt was cool than it was about his customers' ideas. That was his first mistake.

His second mistake was the ensuing marketing campaign to promote Pleasure Cards. He identified 2,000 influential people who he felt could become advocates for his new brand and sent them all customized card samples. With each, he included five free invitations to forward the product to friends and family. His hope was that people would see the cards, love them, and tell other influential people about them. It didn't work.

"Pleasure Cards was too self-centered," Moross openly admits. "It was all about expressing our own brand and not about helping customers express theirs. That miscalculation bled into our marketing. Sending the unsolicited samples came off as too 'spammy.' People hadn't asked for the samples, and it was presumptuous of us to assume they would want them. It actually had an opposite effect from what we had intended. Several people not only threw the cards away, but took the time to tell us not to send them anything else."

Despite this setback, Moross went back to the drawing board and a year later relaunched Pleasure Cards as MOO, the more customer-centric and less "in your face" brand that people know and love today.

Given Moross's design background, the choices that he made in launching Pleasure Cards weren't bad choices. I can imagine being in his shoes and doing exactly what he did. For years, he'd successfully sold his design expertise to clients who loved his work. He had no indication that his design strength might be a weakness in a different situation. As a result, it would have been hard for him to predict failure in advance. He had to fail in order to see the issue for what it was. Ultimately, his greatest strength turned out to be his ability to learn quickly from failure and change course.

In the process of relaunching his site as moo.com in 2006, Moross had another experience that shows how beneficial failure can be. To get the company up and running, he did a marketing deal with photo-sharing site Flickr wherein users could get 10 custom cards for free. Moross was betting that Flickr users, a design-minded community of photographers from around the world, would be an ideal target market for MOO. He was right—almost too right.

In the first week, MOO was flooded by more than 10,000 orders from more than 100 countries. Caught off guard, the company wasn't ready to handle that sort of international demand. Many orders from Asia and the Middle East didn't use the Latin alphabet, which presented a printing problem. Cards were previewing correctly on the screen, but MOO's printing software wasn't capable of handling non-Latin characters, so those orders were printing as all zeros. Several batches of cards were printed and shipped with gibberish before the company caught the problem.

Even worse, when the printing issue was finally resolved, there was the headache of shipping to all those different countries. Moross knew nothing about the massive undertaking of dealing with the taxes and regulations involved in shipping physical goods around the world. He figures that because of the shipping challenges, the company lost money on orders to several countries for months.

Looking back, Moross offers perspective on those early printing and shipping challenges. "We simply had no idea what we were getting ourselves into. While it would have been nice to understand all those challenges in advance, I'm not sure it would have been a smart thing to do. Trying to optimize the business in advance would have cost more and taken longer than just making the mistakes. In a way, failing was more efficient than getting everything right up front."

He adds that the company's early blind spots ended up uncovering some of its best customers. "Had we limited our offering to only a few countries in the beginning, we would have missed out on 10 or 15 of our more successful markets. These are countries that we wouldn't have considered proactively targeting had we not stumbled across them. Success in those markets was a happy accident."

Failing Smarter

The MOO cards story is a good example of why you don't want to avoid failure altogether—it can create fortunate accidents. However, the lesson here isn't that you should go out and just start failing for the sake of failing to see if you can get lucky. Failing can also create a lot of problems if you're not smart about it.

There are no hard and fast rules about what constitutes a smart failure. Some may argue that as long as you don't do yourself any physical harm, all failure is smart because it teaches you something. I tend to see failure as being on a continuum and believe that certain failures are smarter than others. In general, the faster, cheaper, and smaller you fail, while still reaping significant learning, the smarter the failure.

When it comes to starting a business, in order to fail smarter, start-up guru Eric Ries recommends developing a minimum viable product (MVP), the smallest possible product you can create to test your idea and begin to build a following.[1] The key to a good MVP is to keep things simple, testing your core variables quickly. This advice holds for starting just about anything, not just a business.

A few years ago, a friend in the restaurant business shared two case studies that illustrate an MVP and different types of failures well. Both of these stories ended in success. However, the second case was a smarter failure, costing less time, money, and headaches.

In the first case, a woman wanted to open a restaurant using her homemade recipes. She didn't know much about the restaurant business, but her family and friends had loved her cooking for years, so she figured she had what it took to succeed. She put her business plan together, got a loan, and opened her restaurant. Early on, she found out that her recipes weren't as popular as she thought they would be. Reluctantly, she made changes to the menu. She also underestimated the difficulty of building a clientele; people didn't just flock in when she opened the doors the way she thought they would. Trying to learn everything on the fly, from people's tastes to advertising and marketing, she struggled terribly. After three years, she was still not generating enough money to make the restaurant viable, and she shut the doors. Never the quitter, two years later, using the lessons learned from her first failed attempt, she opened a smaller and simpler restaurant that became profitable within a year. While she was glad she'd finally found a path to success, she wished she hadn't lost all that time and money.

In the second case, a different woman, also with a love of cooking yet no formal experience, wanted to open a restaurant. As she was exploring her options, a friend convinced her to sell her cooking at a local farmers' market before taking the bigger plunge. He reasoned that she'd be able to test her recipes for a lot less money. Furthermore, she could build a strong local following for her eventual restaurant before she even opened the doors. She agreed that selling at the farmers' market was a smart idea and rented a commercial kitchen a couple of nights a week to do her cooking. Within a month, she was selling her food at the market. Not having had to build an entire menu and selling only a limited selection each week, she felt freer to test her recipes. Within a year, she had a clear idea of which recipes worked, and she had attracted a loyal clientele. In that time, she had also learned where to buy the best ingredients for the best prices. After giving it another year at the farmers' market, she opened her restaurant. With the momentum she'd built in advance, she was well into the black by the end of her first year in business.

In both of these cases, failures proved beneficial and eventually led to success. However, in the second case, the restaurateur failed smarter because she was able to succeed with a smaller investment of time, money, and energy. By selling her food at the farmers' market instead of opening an entire restaurant, she created an MVP. That allowed her to keep things simple and test two core variables: her recipes and her ability to build a clientele. The first entrepreneur mistakenly thought that she needed a whole restaurant to test those variables. However, the restaurant turned out to be a much less efficient testing ground for failing and learning than the farmers' market was.

Sometimes It Takes Failure to Learn How to Fail Smart

In a way, the second restaurateur in this story is an exception, not the rule. She dodged a tough failure that many risk takers don't or can't dodge early on. Sometimes it's hard to figure out how to fail smart in the beginning, especially if what you're trying to do is new to you.

Yipit.com is a daily deal aggregator. It searches more than 500 daily deal sites, like Groupon and LivingSocial, to find the best deals on the web and sends them to its users based on predefined preferences. There are a few big daily deal aggregators these days, but Yipit is one of the most popular thanks to its broad search of more than 500 sites and its ability to deliver results targeted to specific tastes. The daily deal aggregation service that has made Yipit so popular, and that has attracted millions in venture capital, was started on a whim in a matter of three days, after two carefully planned services failed to get off the ground.

In 2007, Vinicius Vacanti and Jim Moran conceived of Yipit as a local search site for furniture sales in New York City. Leaving their jobs in finance, they took 12 long months to build the original Yipit website, launching it in September 2008. Six months later, with traffic still anemic, they realized that their big idea wasn't going to fly.

Going quickly back to the drawing board, in May 2009 Vacanti and Moran started working on a broader concept, a recommendation engine for all types of deals in New York City. They launched this second iteration of Yipit six months later, in November 2009. Unfortunately, within two months, they realized that they had another dud on their hands. The site wasn't generating the word-of-mouth buzz needed to make it successful.

At this point, in February 2010, two-and-a-half years after starting Yipit and having blown through their savings without having earned a single dollar in revenue, Vacanti and Moran got the idea for the third iteration of the site, an aggregator of other people's deals. While it felt like a good idea, with their confidence at a low point and tired of failing, they had no energy left to pursue it. The prospect of putting their blood, sweat, and tears into yet another failure was unthinkable.

Exhausted and frustrated, they devised a different plan for moving forward: build and launch a smaller test version of the service in three days. Rather than developing a fancy web crawler to search the web for deals, the plan was that they would get up at 3 a.m. every day to search the web for deals themselves. They would then enter the deals they found into their database manually and send a summary e-mail to their users. If the concept took off, they'd worry about building the fancy web crawler later.

They hatched the idea on a Friday, started building it on Sunday, and launched it on Wednesday. By Thursday, they knew that they had a winner on their hands.

People loved the service and immediately started posting it on Twitter. Within a day, *Wired* magazine wrote an article about it. Within a week, Yipit had attracted more users to the site than it had in the past two-and-a-half years combined.

"One of the craziest parts of the story," Vacanti said, "is that within a couple of months, 20 other deal aggregators launched, all with fancy web crawlers. However, the press labeled us the leader in the space because we were first to market. They painted the other aggregators as Yipit copycats, even though several of the other companies had probably had the idea before we did, and definitely had better software at that point. That early jump was our defining competitive advantage."

Vacanti shared another insight that goes to the heart of failing smart. On the Friday they originally developed their idea for the daily deal aggregator, Vacanti and Moran also came up with a list of four reasons why the idea could fail: (1) deal sites (like Groupon) wouldn't allow Yipit to aggregate their deals, (2) deal sites wouldn't pay Yipit enough for sending them deals, (3) the crawler might be too tough to build, and (4) customers might not open the e-mail and/or like it.

"Our big 'aha' was realizing that the fourth reason was the only one that mattered in the beginning," Vacanti explained. "If people didn't like the service, the first three issues were moot points. If people did like the service, we could figure out how to handle the first three issues later. In the past, we would've tried to address all four issues at once and lost the opportunity."

The Yipit success story summarizes the two main lessons of failing early, often, and fast. The first is the importance of identifying the kernel of an idea and quickly testing a limited set of variables as an experiment before wasting a lot of time, money, or energy on it. The second is that, unfortunately, it sometimes takes a long time to learn that first lesson.

Vacanti ended our conversation by acknowledging this paradox of failure. "When I speak with new entrepreneurs, I plead with them to launch early prototypes of their ideas to save their sanity. Yet, in retrospect, I also realize that it took us three years of failure to know exactly what we had to do during those three days in February 2010. In the back of my mind, I know that no matter what I say to a new entrepreneur, he probably needs his own version of our first three years of failure in order to succeed. I just hope, for his sake, that he can do it a little faster."

IDEAS AND TOOLS FOR ACTION

Develop Small Experiments to Test Your Idea

As you consider the risks in front of you, try to isolate key variables to test before putting too much time or money into your idea. The restaurateur experimented with her recipes at the farmers' market before opening her restaurant. Vacanti and Moran experimented with their daily deal e-mail before building the software that would automate it.

It doesn't have to be an entrepreneurial venture. For example, before you buy a big piece of software, are there ways to test your assumptions about its usefulness using Word documents e-mailed around? Or before you start a big marketing campaign, are there simpler ways to reach out to your intended market to test ideas? Whatever your risk, here are some questions to help you frame and build a small experiment.

> ▶ *What's my hypothesis regarding this risk?* For any risk you're thinking about, clarify your hypothesis about why it's a good idea and how you think things are going to work. Getting clear on that first, and writing it down, gives you something broad to test.

▶ *What are the variables that could affect my risk?* Generate a full list of the variables that you believe could affect the risk you're thinking about. These could be your product, competitors, timing, price points, and so on. The bigger the list, the better. The next step will be to prioritize.

▶ *What variables are the most important to test?* Of all the variables you wrote down, which are the most important to test up front? Usually it's assumptions that you made about your product or service, or about the key value that you want to provide.

▶ *How can I test these variables quickly and cheaply?* Sometimes this is obvious and sometimes it isn't. Enlist the help of others to help you consider options.

Define Success Metrics Up Front

What specifically will success look like? This is a simple question, but I've found that far too few people ask or answer it clearly before jumping into a risk.

What are we actually trying to achieve by taking this risk? Are we trying to hit certain sales numbers? Are we trying to generate certain cost savings? Are we trying to attract users? Are we trying to grow at a certain rate? Are we trying to improve our employee engagement numbers? For any of these questions, what specific number are we trying to hit? And if there's no way to measure things quantitatively, how can we measure success qualitatively? Also, in what time frame do we need to deliver results in order for something to be considered a success?

Often people don't define success metrics because sitting down to do so can be a real pain. It requires projecting your risk taking into the future to determine what you must achieve if you are to be successful. The process, however, is important because it allows you to detect missteps and failures early so that you can change course quickly if needed.

As some of the examples in this chapter have demonstrated, you can't always be crystal clear about your success metrics up front.

However, that doesn't mean that you shouldn't try to set them. The process of setting them, learning that you've set the wrong ones, then resetting them can be difficult, but it's productive. What's unproductive is not taking the time to set them thoughtfully in the first place.

Chapter 11 Summary

▶ Failure, while uncomfortable, is essential to progress because it shakes up your thinking and helps you uncover new ideas that you wouldn't have uncovered without a few wrong turns.

▶ Failure also strengthens you by showing you what will and won't work, often doing so in ways that you don't fully understand until you have to draw on the lessons learned at some point down the road.

▶ Not all failures are created equal. Some are smarter than others. In general, the faster, cheaper, and smaller you fail, while still reaping significant learning, the smarter the failure.

▶ One of the keys to failing smart is to keep things simple, picking a few key variables to experiment with and test before doing anything too big. In the entrepreneurial start-up world, Eric Ries has coined the term *minimal viable product* (MVP) to describe this concept.

▶ However, sometimes it takes a few tough failures to learn how to fail smart. You can try to plan the perfect experiments to test an idea before taking a big risk, but that's not always easy to do for a lot of reasons. There will always be variables that you didn't account for. Keeping a learning mentality is your best defense in those situations.

CHAPTER TWELVE

Build Learning
into Everything

*The ability to learn faster than your competitors
may be the only sustainable competitive advantage.*

—ARIE DE GEUS, "Planning as Learning," *Harvard Business
Review*

In 1991, Harvard Business School professor Chris Argyris wrote an article in the *Harvard Business Review* titled "Teaching Smart People How to Learn."[1] Identifying a pervasive and destructive dynamic in organizations, Argyris struck a chord with readers, and the article became one of the most popular of his career.

In it, he argues that smart people are one of the biggest barriers to change and growth in companies, reasoning that because they think they know everything (or think they *should* know everything), they're often particularly bad at learning. Usually without even realizing it, smart people tend to build walls of certainty around themselves, ignoring new information and hindering robust dialogue.

The solution, Argyris suggests, is threefold: (1) become more aware of the fact that you don't know everything and don't have to, (2) be more open to other people questioning your thinking and actions, and (3) be more proactive in questioning other people's thinking and actions. He contends that doing these things creates a more productive environment for learning.

This is good advice. In my experience, Argyris's three suggestions are at the heart of learning in most situations: admit you don't know everything, be more open, and be more inquisitive. Commonsense suggestions, perhaps, but they're far from common practice for several reasons.

First, this type of learning requires vulnerability. To get value from it, you have to expose your thoughts and actions for others to see, possibly admitting that you don't know something or that you have made a mistake. It's much easier to keep quiet and not raise issues.

Second, this kind of learning takes time and energy. Good learning conversations don't happen off the cuff at the water cooler; they require purposeful structure and reflection. Stopping to actually have these conversations can feel like it's getting in the way of getting things done. Reflective conversations are often the first things sacrificed in today's busy organizations.

Last, learning is often poorly planned. Most of us have sat through so-called look back meetings (such as project reviews or postmortems) that merely rehash what everyone already knows. No actionable learning is produced. If you experience enough of these meetings, you soon become skeptical that subsequent meetings will be any different.

So there you are. You're disinclined to enter into learning conversations because they require vulnerability, time, and energy. Then, when you finally find the courage, time, and energy to enter into them, they rarely produce meaningful learning or real change. While you want the conversations to have a powerful impact, you become resigned to the fact that they rarely do.

The result is a vicious cycle of limited learning. It's destructive in normal business conditions. In risk-taking scenarios, where rapid learning is essential, it's downright deadly. On the flip side, if you and your team can get good at having productive learning conversations, it's a competitive advantage that's tough to replicate.

How Learning Happens

When it's taken seriously and structured effectively, learning is more than a casual conversation to discuss what did and didn't go well in a past effort. It digs into *why* things happened and explores implications for the future. Accurate understanding and knowledge are placed ahead of egos. People participate with a desire to truly understand the root causes of their successes and failures so that they know what to repeat and what to change. The conversations may be uncomfortable, but participants realize that the discomfort of getting things out on the table is minimal compared to the pain of making the same mistakes again.

Effective learning conversations can take many forms, but they all share three characteristics: they're structured, simple, and built into everything.

Structured means that the conversations are planned, not ad hoc. It also means that the environment is conducive to exploration and learning; the atmosphere feels open to having frank conversations. Accordingly, all participants take the time to prepare so that they can be fully engaged.

Simple means that the conversations are limited to a manageable number of clear questions and topics, allowing the group to produce useful insights. A simple set of questions also ensures that the conversation can be contained within a realistic time frame. When learning processes get too complex or too lengthy, people instinctively want to avoid them. Even if learning is ultimately produced, the process feels too painful and too onerous.

Built into everything means that learning processes are woven throughout the execution of an initiative, not just once it's complete. This produces learning *in* action, not just *after* action, which allows for real-time adjustment of plans, helping you get better faster (which is critical during risk taking). It also helps keep learning conversations focused on important issues because you're not trying to cover everything in one marathon meeting. Lastly, because the learning conversations are more frequent, it builds the muscle to have more of them. A natural outgrowth is increased trust among the members of a team.

One of the most effective processes for structured, simple, and built-into-everything learning is *debriefing*. Originating in the military as a way to learn quickly in battle, debriefing has gained traction in a wide variety of organizations over the last few decades because its commonsense approach makes it easy to understand and adopt. Here are a few examples of debriefing in action and how it generates timely, crucial learning.

Helping a Pro Football Team Win a Super Bowl

At week six of the 2011 National Football League season, New York Giants head coach Tom Coughlin was looking to give his team an edge. The team was off to a decent start at 4–2, but it had a tough schedule ahead of it. A veteran coach, Coughlin knew that the edge wouldn't come from glaringly obvious changes he could make at the individual level. He already had a team of world-class athletes and coaches who wanted to win a Super Bowl more than anything. He also knew that in the NFL, world-class talent isn't an edge; it's table stakes. He needed something to help the team come together as a high-performing unit.

Figuring that military experience would resonate with his players, Coughlin invited Jim Murphy, Jim Demarest, and Scott Taylor from Afterburner, a training firm of former elite pilots and soldiers, to address the team on leadership and execution. He reasoned that in both sports and military situations, teams are making split-second decisions under pressure, and tiny changes can make the difference between winning and losing (or, in the case of the military, living and dying).

During the Giants' bye week, Murphy and his colleagues took the players and coaches through the Afterburner process of Flawless Execution: plan, brief, execute, and debrief.[2] The team enjoyed the whole presentation, but the last element landed most powerfully. As the consultants described productive debriefing—*a set time and place; nameless and rankless; open and honest, no finger-pointing; objectives reviewed and analyzed; and lessons learned codified with clear implications for the future—* the team members realized that they were bad at it. As a result, they weren't learning and improving fast enough. Even worse, they were missing opportunities to support one another and strengthen the team.

"I was shocked," Murphy admitted after spending the first day with the team. "If any organization was going to be as good at debriefing as the military, I would have figured it was an NFL team, given the high-stakes environment these teams operate in. But they weren't. Like many of my corporate clients, these guys had process gaps all over the place. They were letting critical learning just fall through the cracks."

Over the coming weeks, Murphy, Demarest, and Taylor worked with coaches, offense, and defense to help them get better at debriefing. In particular, they helped team members improve their root-cause analysis, moving beyond identifying mistakes to understanding why the mistakes were happening.

Murphy shared the following example to illustrate the issue. "In so many football locker rooms, you hear comments like, 'Smith, you missed that tackle; don't miss it again.' The trouble with comments like this is that Smith may have missed the tackle because of two or three things that other people weren't doing well. Just telling Smith to make the tackle next time doesn't solve the other problems. And if those problems don't get solved, chances are that Smith is going to miss the tackle again. This is the type of environment we found when we started working with the team."

Murphy's example is a classic case of poor feedback that produces little valuable learning. Neither Smith nor the rest of the team is walking out of that locker room any smarter or better than when he walked in.

To make root-cause analysis work, a team has to get rid of the tendency to point fingers. Instead of saying, "Smith, you missed that tackle," the team needs to get better at asking, "Why did Smith miss that tackle?" and discussing it together. This requires the team to recognize that Smith's missing the tackle isn't just his problem, it's a team problem, and several forces may have caused it.

Effective root-cause analysis also requires that members feel comfortable admitting errors. A locker room full of players who are trying to cover up their mistakes out of fear of reprimand is a useless debriefing environment that rarely gets to root causes. The best way to get started is to have senior members of the team role-model the behavior for the younger, less experienced players, who might be more fearful.

"In the first offensive debriefing, I asked [quarterback] Eli Manning to share where he had made a mistake or missed an opportunity to achieve a specific team goal," Murphy explained, saying that Manning was a natural for these kinds of conversations. "He did it without missing a beat. It opened up the room and changed the environment. Soon everyone felt comfortable talking about his mistakes."

Before long, the team was proactively dissecting plays together, freely admitting places where they could improve instead of waiting for a coach to do something. In fact, the players saw more opportunities for improvement than the coaches could ever see because there were simply more analytical eyes reviewing the games. The environment was also nameless and rankless, meaning that anyone could point out any issue regardless of who was involved, even if it was a coach or a more senior player. Learning, not position, was of paramount importance; egos had to be checked at the door.

The team continued to practice these new debriefings for the rest of the season, through ups and downs, through the playoffs, and eventually to a Super Bowl ring. After their big win, Eli Manning and linebacker Mathias Kiwanuka were interviewed by Damon Hack for an article in *Sports Illustrated*, and the topic of debriefing came up.[3]

Asked what made the debriefing sessions work so well, Manning said, "I wasn't coaching anybody. I was just coaching myself, looking at what I needed to do better and telling everybody. Then everybody would talk about what they needed to do to improve."

Kiwanuka saw a direct connection between debriefing and the world-class team that won the championship. "There was a time there when we needed every single minute of [debriefing]," he said. "It wasn't about calling people out.

It was an opportunity to see everybody hold themselves accountable. The big part of why we're here is that fingers don't get pointed. These kinds of teams don't come along very often."

It makes you wonder, did a world-class team choose to do debriefing, or did debriefing create a world-class team? I bet it was a bit of both.

Preparing Soldiers for a New Type of War

In 2003, Colonel Joseph A. Moore used rapid learning to develop a very different type of world-class team: a mock insurgency that would train U.S. Army forces being deployed to the Middle East.

Since 1982, the U.S. Army National Training Center, located in the Mojave Desert, has been preparing soldiers for battle by re-creating real-life field conditions. For the first 20 years of its existence, that amounted to Soviet-style tank battles. Each month, the 11th Armored Cavalry Regiment (ACR) would play the enemy (known as the opposing force or OPFOR), challenging visiting units from the army, the reserves, or the National Guard in classic tank-on-tank warfare. The idea was to re-create the feeling of two professional armies trying to defeat each other.

In 2003, things changed. Following the invasions of Afghanistan and Iraq, the army found itself up against a new kind of enemy and a new kind of warfare. Rather than large, organized militaries, the new threats were insurgent forces hiding among civilian populations. Warfare had become a more nuanced and delicate proposition.

To prepare soldiers for this new reality, Colonel Joseph Moore, commander of OPFOR, was given two enormous jobs: (1) transform the Mojave Desert into realistic Middle Eastern towns to create the proper setting, and (2) retrain the 11th ACR to act like a completely different opposing force. To make his job more difficult, he didn't have much time to get either of these jobs done. With the conflicts in the Middle East escalating quickly, he had to start training people within months.

"To give you an idea of how big the physical job alone was," Moore explained, "we had to construct nine Middle Eastern villages from scratch in four weeks. We took our entire tank budget and started buying buildings and sheds. As well, we hired every contractor who could construct a building in 30 days."

As daunting as that sounds, in many ways the construction was the easier of the two jobs. Retraining 2,500 cavalry soldiers to realistically think and act like insurgents and Middle Eastern civilians was a much bigger challenge.

"These soldiers had been trained for years to operate tanks and heavy weapons on the battlefield, and now we were asking them to put on traditional Afghan or Iraqi robes and pretend to be merchants with no military training," said Moore. "As you might imagine, the first few times through the exercise, the soldiers had no idea how to act."

Enter the army's *after action review* (AAR) process.[4]

Similar to the debriefing used by Afterburner with the New York Giants, an AAR is a method of getting mistakes and successes out on the table quickly, identifying root causes, and reapplying learning to future action. Normally Moore's OPFOR used AARs to get better in battle. Now they were using them to get better at role playing. The more closely OPFOR could re-create actual conditions, the better prepared the troops would be.

Moore described just how "real-time" the operation was. "We were getting new information daily, watching the news and talking to colleagues on the ground in Afghanistan and Iraq. We were given permission to change anything we saw fit as we watched the conditions in the theater develop. To do that, we had to be in constant communication, integrating new knowledge at all times in order to add more realistic nuance."

One example of an important nuance that was perfected through AARs was figuring out how to accurately portray things like gunfire in public places, something that the troops would inevitably have to deal with in the field.

"The first time shots were fired in our simulations, my OPFOR 'enemy civilians' retreated in an orderly fashion to the same place," Moore said. "It looked utterly ridiculous. That's not how civilians act. Civilians start pushing and shoving, literally running over each other in a chaotic frenzy. It took four or five AARs and a couple of rehearsals over a week's time before we created the chaos we needed. Eventually we even recruited 500 U.S. citizens of Middle Eastern descent to live at the base and be part of the simulations. There were hundreds of examples like this."

All told, it took a month to build nine villages, a couple of months to train OPFOR to be "good enough" to simulate insurgents and start running classes, and another six months to "perfect" key elements of OPFOR's new guerrilla approach. It was remarkably fast given the number of people and moving parts involved.

"Transforming the desert and retraining OPFOR in such a short time frame was the most challenging thing I did in my more than 30 years in the army," Moore said.

The experience strengthened his belief in the power of tools like the AAR to help teams improve in fast-changing situations. "When we were still doing Soviet-style tank battles, we had gotten into a habit of doing AARs only when we needed them, perhaps every few weeks when something went wrong. But in the thick of the new changes, I needed to be in an AAR every 48 hours to debrief, learn, and integrate lessons. That meant that the soldiers below me were doing AARs several times a day to gain the insights they needed in order to improve. Without the constant AARs, there's no way we could have done what we did, let alone that quickly."

The process also reminded Moore that good AARs should be about acknowledging and learning from successes as much as from mistakes. "One of my captains had done a great job on something, and I wanted to use an AAR to learn from it. When he heard I had called an AAR, he was crushed, assuming that the focus would be on mistakes he'd made. It made me realize that we'd gotten out of balance and hadn't been learning from our successes enough. The process has to focus on both the ups and the downs to be motivating and useful."

Rapid Learning During the Pilot Stage of a Project

Sports teams and the military provide easy examples to illustrate learning in action because they're fast-paced environments with a lot of variables at play. The same can be said of most business situations.

Chapter 8 introduced DaVita, the kidney dialysis provider that dramatically improved insurance coverage by creating a more proactive and intimate approach to working with patients. In early 2012, a year after starting the pilot, the insurance management team's (IMT's) new approach was working like a finely oiled machine. The team had figured out how to prioritize cases and focus on the ones it could help most. It had gotten intake questionnaires down to the most critical information. And it had clear timing guidelines to help insurance counselors provide great service, yet not burn themselves out.

As is often the case with highly effective business processes, the new approach looked like a simple procedure brainstormed by the group over a few weeks. In reality, it took constant trial and error along with weekly debriefings over six months to make the new approach really work.

At the outset of the pilot, the team members had a good idea of the new processes they would need. However, as they started executing, they learned that the devil was in the details, and that getting it right was going to take a lot of shared learning. For example, the group started with 15 questions on the intake form, but this quickly ballooned to 70 questions as people thought of additional pieces of patient information that would be helpful to know. Realizing that 70 questions was too many, yet not wanting to make arbitrary cuts, pilot team members spent several months sharing insights gleaned from specific conversations with patients in order to narrow the list to the most helpful questions. This type of debriefing and continuous learning was happening at all levels of the pilot.

"Two things in particular made our debriefing work," IMT director Jud Dean said. "The first was that we took the time to clarify specific objectives in terms of revenue and patients served. Nothing was nebulous. Every action we took could be measured against those objectives and whether it was helping or hindering us. Debriefing also worked because the insurance counselors 'in the trenches' were involved in debriefings too, not just their supervisors. This ensured that detailed insights made their way into the learning for everyone to hear."

Dean admitted that this second success factor is an easy one to miss in today's fast-paced business culture. "As a director, it would have been easier for me to just check in with the supervisors below me rather than having biweekly calls with the whole team. In a business-as-usual environment, using quick check-ins can work. However, in an environment where you're trying to make big changes and take risks, the detailed debriefings and learning are important to success."

To make the debriefings effective, Dean adopted a simple structure for the calls, covering five questions each time. (1) What were our objectives over the last two weeks? (2) What were our successes? (3) What should we watch out for? (4) What key insights did we glean? (5) What are our recommendations for the future? All team members were expected to participate actively. After each debriefing, a one-page synopsis of the call was distributed as part of a document that contained notes from all past debriefings. This allowed team members to see their progress and ensure that they were integrating new learning into their actions over the following two weeks.

Therese Lineweaver, an insurance counselor in the pilot, described a key force that motivated the rapid learning. "We were 6 people piloting new processes for 150 other people who would have to live with whatever we created. We felt a real responsibility to get it right, which meant pushing ourselves outside our comfort zone sometimes. We were very honest about what worked and what didn't. We kept asking questions. Can we add this? Or take this away? Or change this element to streamline things more?"

"It was a lot of hard work," said Shannon Oswalt, another insurance counselor, "but we created a much more proactive and innovative approach to insurance management as a result. I don't think anyone else in the dialysis world is doing what we're doing."

With the pilot completed and the new processes being rolled out through 2012, Dean has made the debriefing process a core part of ongoing management. "We continue to deep-dive for our most successful wins every month using the same five questions," he said. "We then regularly share the learning with insurance counselors in the field to help them continually get better at what they do."

IDEAS AND TOOLS FOR ACTION

At its core, productive learning is a mindset. More than a set of questions or actions, it's an understanding that, in the grand scheme of things, no one person knows very much. Taking this simple truth to heart creates an openness to learning. Conversely, holding on to the illusion that you know more than you do tends to shut down learning. In order to learn more, let go of the need to look smart all the time. I often tell clients that genuine confidence doesn't come from knowing what you're doing; it comes from realizing that no one really knows what she's doing. And genuine confidence is an important part of creating a learning mindset.

Debriefing

A productive debriefing has four elements. It can be done in as little as 10 minutes or take as long as several hours, depending on the size and scope of what's being debriefed. I've found that 30 to 60 minutes is optimal for harvesting learning and keeping the conversation focused.

Schedule the Time and Place

The key here is to make the debriefing expected, putting everyone in a learning mindset from the beginning of an activity. People know that they're going to be getting together, and they know what the general structure of the conversation will be, which helps them begin gathering insights in advance of the process. Eventually, the more you debrief, the more effective and efficient it becomes.

Create a Learning Environment

Expectations should be set that it's learning that's front and center, not position in the organization. The expression the army uses is *leave your stripes at the door*. The most senior leaders in the room set the tone. When they make themselves vulnerable and admit the errors they've made, it gives everyone else permission to do so too.

Another key aspect of creating the right learning environment is not pointing fingers. The results, both good and bad, should be considered team results, recognizing that everyone had a hand in creating them.

Review Four Key Questions

This is the heart of a good debriefing. The same four questions should be reviewed in every debriefing, regardless of length.

1. What Were We Trying to Accomplish (Objectives)?

Every debriefing should start by restating the objectives you were trying to hit. The group should have agreed on clear objectives prior to taking action in the first place. If there's a lack of clarity here, the rest of the debriefing will be of little value because you won't know how to judge your success.

For example, generating five wins when you had an initial objective of three will lead to a very different learning conversation from generating five wins when you had an initial objective of fifteen. In the former, you're trying to figure out why you did so well and how to tweak around the edges. In the latter, you're trying to figure out why you did so poorly and what larger changes need to be made.

In my experience, teams are often bad at setting objectives early on, especially if the initiative is at a conceptual or strategic phase. Pushing yourself to do this is important in setting the stage for learning and rapid improvement.

2. Where Did We Hit Our Objectives or Miss Our Objectives?

When you have clear objectives, this is a pretty straightforward conversation, as you either did or didn't hit them. Review your results and ensure that the group is aligned.

3. What Caused Our Results?

This is the root-cause analysis, and it should go deeper than obvious, first-level answers. For example, if you were trying to generate fifteen wins and you generated only five, don't be satisfied with answers like, "We didn't try hard enough." Keep digging and ask *why* you didn't try hard enough.

Are you overwhelmed because the team hasn't prioritized its work? Are incentives misguided, so that people don't feel motivated to try harder? Is the task too complex, so that people are giving up too easily? There are many reasons why people don't try hard enough. If you don't get to the root cause, you can't create actionable learning for the future.

An effective tool for root-cause analysis is "five whys." For every answer you give, ask why that's the case. By the time you've answered the question five times, you've usually uncovered some fundamental issues that are holding you back.

4. What Should We Start, Stop, or Continue Doing?

Given the root causes that were uncovered, what does that mean for behavior change? Specifically, what should we start, stop, or continue doing now that we know what we know?

Codify Lessons Learned

Make sure that you capture lessons learned in a usable format for later reference and use. At a minimum, this involves taking notes and distributing them to the members present. Other methods can make the information more readily available to a broader audience. For example, at Procter & Gamble, R&D professionals submit Smart Learning Reports (SLRs) to a database, based on monthly research lessons learned, that can be searched by anyone in R&D worldwide.

Chapter 12 Summary

▶ The further you get in your career and the smarter you get at what you're doing, the tougher it can be to learn. This can have a negative impact on your ability to grow and improve yourself or your organization.

▶ In order to stay open to learning, (1) become more aware of the fact that you don't know everything and don't have to, (2) be more open to other people questioning your thinking and actions, and (3) be more proactive in questioning other people's thinking and actions.

▶ Effective learning conversations are structured, simple, and built into everything you do.

▶ An example of an effective learning conversation is a *debriefing*. Used by the military as a way to learn quickly in battle, debriefing has gained traction in a wide variety of organizations over the last few decades because it's a commonsense approach that's easy to understand and adopt.

▶ In addition to the military, sports teams such as the New York Giants and businesses such as DaVita have used debriefings to learn and improve quickly.

▶ Key elements of a productive debriefing are that it's scheduled, people at all levels feel safe and open to share their thoughts, it gets to the root causes of issues, and it codifies learning for future use.

Stay Humble

*When you get overconfident, that's when something
snaps up and bites you.*
—**NEIL ARMSTRONG,** 2004 CNN interview

The Greek philosopher Heraclitus famously said, "No man ever steps in the same river twice." No matter what river we stepped in yesterday, today brings different water, different currents, and different conditions—in essence, a different river.

The smartest risk takers have a deep understanding of and respect for this idea. They realize that even if they masterfully crossed one river yesterday, today is a different day. It brings just as many challenges, and sometimes even more, because the more success you have, the less vigilant you become.

To be a humble risk taker requires managing a fundamental tension between conviction and doubt. You must simultaneously make a decision to move, yet realize that you may be wrong. Conviction without doubt leads to overconfidence and loss of control. Doubt without conviction leads to paralysis and inaction. Smart risk takers balance both.

The following three stories show how humility leads to smarter action, smarter learning, and smarter risk taking.

Keep Following the Questions

As CEO of the Energy Project, a multimillion-dollar training company focused on helping people and companies fuel more sustainable high performance, Tony Schwartz has been a trusted advisor to top executives at Google, Apple, Sony, Ford, and Ernst & Young, among many other companies. He founded his firm in 2003, after coauthoring the *New York Times* bestseller *The Power of Full Engagement*. He knew that book was a hit when Oprah Winfrey invited him and his coauthor, Jim Loehr, to be on her show and proclaimed that everyone who was watching should read the book.

The Energy Project is the latest in a long list of risks that Schwartz has had pay off during his career. In the mid-1970s, when he was just out of college, Schwartz left a job writing a column about politics to become the gossip columnist for the *New York Post*. While this move garnered him more exposure, most people considered it a step in the wrong direction for a serious journalist. Against the odds, he figured out how to parlay the *New York Post* column into subsequent jobs at *Newsweek*, *New York* magazine, and the *New York Times*, building a solid journalistic reputation along the way. He put that at risk again by choosing to coauthor Donald Trump's 1988 bestseller, *The Art of the Deal*. Next, Schwartz walked away from a range of more lucrative book offers and instead spent several years searching for something deeper in life, culminating in his 1996 book, *What Really Matters*. It was through researching this book that Schwartz met Jim Loehr, a world-renowned performance psychologist. Six years later, they coauthored *The Power of Full Engagement*. Later that same year, Schwartz parted ways with Loehr and started over from scratch by founding the Energy Project. Initially it was just him and his assistant.

Interestingly, after all his success, Schwartz will be the first to tell you that he doesn't feel he's figured everything out.

"The more I do, the more I realize how little I know," Schwartz said, reflecting on his career so far. "I don't have the answers. I just keep following the questions and sharing the insights I stumble on. My curiosity has built a great business and a wonderful life, but I'm careful not to mistake insights for certainty. It would kill my ability to learn and grow."

Schwartz's learning mentality was on display during a day-long strategy meeting I spent with his company in early 2011. The meeting's primary focus was to plan for the next year.

However after a tough 2010, the team members felt that they needed to start by reviewing the past year's challenges for lessons learned.

Each person shared thoughts on his/her personal mistakes, group mistakes, and implications for the future. Schwartz went first, revealing some significant miscalculations he felt he'd made and the negative impact they had had. He ended with a heartfelt apology.

As others shared their thoughts, the dialogue got heated. Some of the most pointed comments were directed squarely at Schwartz. The comments were clearly difficult for him to hear, yet throughout he listened closely, trying to truly understand the frustrations. He inquired a few times for clarification, but other than that, he said very little.

Eventually the conversation turned away from Schwartz and toward a shared sense of responsibility. Others acknowledged mistakes that they had made and areas where they wanted to do better. Two hours later, the conversation ended in a fairly productive place.

David Covey, son of the famed personal development guru Stephen Covey, happened to be in the meeting that day because he was working on a project for the Energy Project. Watching the dialogue unfold, Covey commented that he was struck by Schwartz's vulnerability and composure throughout the difficult conversation. Covey added that he wasn't sure his father would have been able to listen to and digest a conversation like that.

Schwartz was grateful that the conversation happened, sharing his takeaway with the team. "Sometimes I get really focused and passionate about an idea and push hard for it. In the process, I can inadvertently exclude other perspectives. While I've always known I have this tendency, the conversation today really helped me see how negative the impact can be."

Thanking everyone, he committed to staying open to conversations like this in the future.

"This is where the real learning happens," Schwartz said with a smile and a little exhaustion. "Let's just wait a few weeks before we do it again."

Don't Be a Hero

For Tony Schwartz, humility puts him in a better position to grow his company in the long term. In certain businesses, humility is required just to stay alive.

Wall Street is rarely considered a humble place, especially since the financial crisis of 2008. To many, the industry is rife with egotistical and reckless professionals. Having spent a fair amount of time with people on Wall Street, I can't say the reputation is totally unfounded.

At the same time, some of the sharpest, most thoughtful risk managers I've ever met have been on Wall Street. These are people who did well before the financial crisis and have done well since it. You rarely hear about them because they tend to keep low profiles.

The Wall Street firms I know best, and have worked with the most, are institutional money managers. These firms invest money for endowments, pension funds, and insurance companies, among other large organizations. This kind of business is one of the most attractive in finance because the payoff for success is extremely high. However, it's also one of the most brutal because the price of failure is equally high; a couple of bad years usually means the end of your career, often before it ever gets started.

Talented money managers usually have a high degree of intelligence, an analytical mind, and a steely set of nerves. These skills help them identify new ideas, pick them apart, develop conviction as to whether or not to invest, and then make strategic decisions.

Unfortunately, having talent isn't enough to succeed in money management, a business that is littered with talented people who've been chewed up and spit out in the blink of an eye. Veteran money managers will tell you that the difference between the talented managers who succeed and the talented managers who don't is *humility*.

The archetypal downfall of a talented money manager often goes something like this. The manager makes a few good investments and starts to feel confident. His ego grows, and he mistakenly starts to think he's smarter than other people. Before long, believing that he has a golden touch, he starts taking irresponsible risks, not giving himself room for error if a trade turns bad. He isn't worried because he's confident that he's right. Eventually, one of his trades turns bad. That fact alone isn't a problem; everyone has bad trades. His problem is that because of his ego, he bets too much too fast on that single trade, trying to hit a home run. He ends up losing tons of money, sending his portfolio into an unrecoverable tailspin, and putting himself out of business, thus making it nearly impossible for him to ever get back in the game. In the end, it's not his mistake that brought him down; it's the fact that he thought he couldn't make one.

"Don't be a hero. Don't have an ego. Always question yourself and your ability. Don't ever feel that you are very good. The second you do, you are dead." This is advice from legendary investor Paul Tudor Jones in a 1987 PBS interview after he successfully navigated the Black Monday stock market crash. Twenty-five years later, Tudor Jones is still among the most successful money managers in the world. Asked in that same interview, "When did you turn from a loser to a winner in your investments?" Jones answered, "When I was able to accept being wrong."

"The best investment managers are wrong about 45 percent of the time," said Dan Sundheim, a top money manager who also happens to be my cousin. "That's the nature of our business, but a lot of people struggle with that fact. They think they have a brilliant 'can't lose' idea, and it blinds them in really destructive ways. They might bet too big on it. Or they might stay in a position long after they should have gotten out of it. They lose their objectivity and judgment because they find it hard to admit that they might have made a bad call."

It's a recurring theme you hear from longtime money managers. Overconfidence is the kiss of death. When interviewing people for his fund, it's one of the first things Sundheim has his antennae up for.

"We're looking for people who can have strong, insightful ideas while simultaneously being open to the possibility that they're wrong," he explained. "It might seem contradictory, but it's a really important tension for people to be able to manage. If people can't challenge their own assumptions or aren't open to other people challenging their assumptions, it's usually a bad sign."

Sundheim makes a point of challenging his own thoughts and strategies daily. Even if he feels that his analysis of a new idea is spot on, he actively seeks in-depth critical feedback from his team and his peers.

"Thoroughly pulling apart an idea and looking at it from every angle is the only way to get the detailed insights we need to make smart decisions," Sundheim explained. "There's no room for big egos. If one of us makes a bad bet, it affects all of us."

Shine the Spotlight on Others

Investment funds like Sundheim's are nimble organizations that can make and execute decisions on a dime. In larger companies, decisions can take months or years to play out. Humility is equally important in these scenarios.

In Chapter 5, you heard about how CEO Mike Waite and his leadership team rebuilt Menasha Packaging after a failed sale. Within 12 months of its near-death experience, the company had retooled its product offering, reignited a fighting spirit among its employees, and significantly increased revenue and profit. In the years that followed, it was much the same story—happier and happier clients and increasingly strong financials.

After presiding over a turnaround like Menasha's, some CEOs might stand up and take credit for the success. Frankly, who could blame them? It's a tough job filled with a lot of battle scars. Other, more understated CEOs might graciously accept congratulations on the results and not make a big deal of it. And then there's Mike Waite, who's done neither.

"Mike is one of the most humble leaders I've ever met," said Deb Mills-Scofield, a consultant who's worked with Menasha since 2005 and helped facilitate some of the planning that's gotten it to where it is today. "The turnaround Mike has led has been nothing short of remarkable. There were so many ways this operation could have failed, and yet, against the odds, not only has it survived, but it's thriving. The collaborative, supportive, results-oriented culture that Mike has cultivated is a big part of the reason why. You'd never get him to acknowledge that, though."

To Waite, the organization below him does the heavy lifting. All he does is make sure that nothing gets in people's way as they experiment, learn, and make the business better. It's the members of his team and their teams that deserve the credit, not him.

One example of a big win under Waite's leadership is the Retail Integration Institute (RII). Spearheaded by Jeff Krepline and Jerry Hessel in early 2005, it aimed to give Menasha an edge by providing advisory support, not just corrugated boxes, to consumer packaged goods (CPG) companies. Krepline and Hessel figured that Menasha's extensive knowledge of packaging, competitive CPG shelf strategies, and the needs of retailers would be valuable to its customers. By building a consulting team of marketing specialists, Menasha could reposition itself as a more thoughtful solution provider.

Some members of the Menasha leadership and board were skeptical at first. They figured that RII would merely add costs to a product that already had razor-thin margins. However, as Waite saw the dynamics of the industry changing, he knew that the only way to survive was to go upmarket and give clients more strategic value. With that in mind, Waite gave Krepline and Hessel the air cover and resources they needed to make a go of it.

Krepline and Hessel hired designers and retail specialists immediately. Within 18 months, they had chalked up significant wins with SC Johnson and Kimberly-Clark, both of which found RII's thought partnership to be invaluable. With the idea validated, RII grew quickly, becoming a leading sales engine for the company.

When board members congratulated Waite on a job well done, his knee-jerk response was to deflect it, taking none of the credit. In his eyes, RII was Krepline and Hessel's baby, and they and their teams deserved all the praise. Seven years later, Waite still refuses to take any credit for bringing RII to life.

Since then, Menasha has taken many more risks and launched many more great ideas. For each, Waite tells the same story: he didn't do much beyond getting out of the way and letting great people do their thing.

While consultant Mills-Scofield wishes that Waite would take a little more credit for the great things that Menasha has accomplished, she admits that his approach has a powerful impact on the organization. "Mike's humility has a way of opening people up and getting ideas and conversations flowing. People don't feel like they're going to be judged. He sets the boundaries, but then gets out of the way to let people take risks, rapidly iterate, and learn. People also know that if they do something well, they're going to get the credit for it. There's no hogging the limelight."

Mills-Scofield raises an important point regarding the power of humility in leaders. It's more than merely being disarming and easygoing. Humble leaders tend to create an environment that's conducive to smart risk taking by setting the field of play, giving power away to others, and then stepping back to let great things happen.

IDEAS AND TOOLS FOR ACTION

In many ways, humility is a natural outgrowth of weathering the inevitable ups and downs of life. The following suggestions are small things you can do on a regular basis to cultivate humility. They go a long way toward creating the space for productive learning.

Appreciate the Efforts of Others

Appreciating the efforts of others is a powerful way to cultivate humility. Much of the value of the process comes from taking the time to think about other people, something we can fail to do when life gets hectic. By getting out of your own head and into someone else's, you're reminded that it's not all about you.

Opportunities to appreciate others can be formal, such as awards and bonuses, but they don't have to be. Just as powerful are informal opportunities such as acknowledgment in meetings, a quick e-mail of thanks, or a handwritten note (not something that people do much anymore, which gives it a more powerful impact).

The power of appreciation tends to sneak up on you. When you initially start doing it, you don't think much of it. Then, as you do it more and more, you see a shift in how you're perceiving people. You understand their struggles, hard work, failures, and successes, which makes you appreciate them more.

Listen Twice as Much as You Talk

You can learn more by listening than by talking. Yet even knowing this, it's easy to get stuck in a rut, talking too much and missing opportunities to learn. You might feel you've got something really great to say. Or you might feel smarter than others on a particular topic. Or you might think that someone doesn't understand your point, so you have to keep repeating it until he gets it. Whatever the reason, we all fall victim to talking too much at times. We just want to be heard.

Occasionally talking a lot is not a problem; mathematically, not everyone can listen twice as much as she talks in all conversations. It becomes a problem only when you do it too much, ending up stuck in your own perspective and deaf to good information around you.

The best advice is to start paying attention to the conversations you're in. Are you listening more than you're talking, or vice versa? While the ratio changes depending on the audience and the situation, a 2-to-1 listening-to-talking ratio is a good proxy for humility. It means that you're open to others' thinking, getting in their shoes and really understanding them. At the same time, you're finding the right opportunities to share your thinking, testing it and making it better.

Chapter 13 Summary

► Heraclitus' famous line, "No man ever steps in the same river twice," reminds us that no matter how much we know, circumstances change, and that we should bring a humble, curious mind to all that we do.

▶ Being a humble risk taker requires managing a fundamental tension between conviction and doubt. Too much of one without the other creates either overconfidence or paralysis.

▶ Even if we feel that others have less experience than we do, it's important that we take the time to listen to them because they have *different* experiences from ours, and we can learn from their perspective.

▶ The most successful risk takers expect that they're going to be wrong a fair amount of the time and put valid information and learning ahead of their egos.

▶ Humble leaders tend to create an environment that's conducive to smart risk taking by setting the field of play, giving power away to others, and then stepping back to let great things happen.

PART FIVE

COMMUNICATE POWERFULLY

Expect Communication to Break Down

The single biggest problem in communication is the illusion that it has taken place.

—GEORGE BERNARD SHAW

When it comes to pursuing new ideas, entering new markets, or trying to make any big changes that involve other people, I always tell clients to start with the assumption that their communication is going to break down. This advice isn't based on my observations of them, their specific organization, or the specific situation they're facing. Rather, it's based on my observations of hundreds of leaders just like them, all their organizations, and all the situations they've faced. Whenever two or more people are involved in *anything*, there's a good chance that communication will break down at some point.

I see it in my own life and business. While it's my job to help leaders and teams get better at communicating, and I'm hyperaware of pitfalls that can lead to poor communication, I still have communication breakdowns. I might get busy and not let other team members know what I'm doing. Or I might spend so much time thinking about a topic that I forget that others aren't on the same page as I am. Or I might not share a piece of information because it doesn't occur to me that it would be helpful for others to know it. Given the pace of business today, it's easy for these things to happen, even when I know better.

Recognizing how easily breakdowns can occur, I have weekly check-in meetings with my team on key projects. When an issue rears its head, we'll discuss why it happened, how to address it, and how to avoid it in the future. However, although we get better, we never completely eliminate communication breakdowns. Invariably, a different issue under different circumstances arises several months later, and we'll go through the process again.

I've come to see communication breakdowns as a simple fact of human interaction and organizational life, especially when you're up to something big. There are always a lot of moving parts to manage. If you expect breakdowns, catch them, and address them, you can lessen their frequency, intensity, and negative impact. Also, if you deepen your appreciation for why they happen, you can get better at predicting them in advance.

The Communication Blind Spot

Communication within organizations breaks down for many complex reasons, ranging from power dynamics to low levels of trust to hidden agendas. However, in my experience, the most common reason communication breaks down is much simpler than these. It happens because people fail to realize that they have information that should be communicated in a more focused, thoughtful, and frequent way.

I call this the communication blind spot. It frequently unfolds something like this. People get together, talk about something over a number of months, and come to a set of decisions. Then they share their decisions with a few people in the organization in an ad hoc fashion. They might even send a document around outlining the decision. Three months later, because they've been talking about the issue so much and they remember sending a document around, they're under the illusion that everyone understands and appreciates the decision the same way that they do. They're blinded to the fact that others, who weren't in the original planning meetings and have never been focused on the ideas that the planners discussed, don't have nearly the same appreciation for those ideas. Then one of the original planners brings up the idea in a meeting, assuming that everyone is on the same page as he is. Unfortunately, 75 percent of the room has no idea what he's talking about. The person bringing it up can't believe it. He was sure that the decision and rationale were shared very clearly with the organization months ago. But he was wrong.

The communication blind spot happens because once something becomes really clear to us, we have a tendency to think that it's clear to everyone else, too. As a result, we don't feel that the topic needs a lot of detailed communication. That's when problems begin. People have different understandings of the issue. They draw different conclusions, and they begin operating from different sets of assumptions.

Following are three examples of how communication can break down, the role the communication blind spot plays, and specific strategies for strengthening communication.

Bringing a Company Back to Life

In Chapter 5, I mentioned that in order to signal that they were serious about the strategic changes they were making, CEO Mike Waite and his leadership team at Menasha put a premium on strong communication. They visited every plant at eight complexes around the United States to personally share the new strategy and get feedback. This was the most visible demonstration of their commitment to the path forward. At the same time, they used a variety of other tactics to help clarify why the changes were important and what everyone needed to do on the road ahead. Menasha's approach provides a good case study in how to communicate when trust is low, the stakes are high, and everyone has to change.

"We did a lot of strategic planning," Waite said, looking back on the process. "Yet the leadership team agreed that success wasn't going to be about having the best strategy. It was going to be about executing it. And the heart of great execution is great communication."

An important first step was the team's acknowledging that historically it hadn't been great at communication. The team members had tended to rely on ad hoc opportunities to share information throughout the company. New strategies would be generated with no obvious communication plan. While there was a general expectation that VPs would share important information with general managers, general managers would share it with managers, and managers would share it with all other employees, the process was too undefined to work well. Messages got delivered incorrectly, partially, and sometimes not at all. People on the plant floors didn't get to hear directly from senior leaders. Going forward, with so much on the line, Waite and his team knew that this would have to change.

To get everyone on the same page, the team created a formal communication plan for the coming year. It clarified how the changes were going to affect different groups, and it identified what messages each group needed to hear, and at what times. It also outlined a variety of new communication vehicles, including videos and newsletters, that would be used to increase the likelihood that people would receive and understand the information. Built into the plan were opportunities for constant feedback from all organizational levels to ensure that communication was moving in both directions. Once the plan was done, the leaders were quick to get messages out, starting to communicate less than a week after they had clarified the strategy.

One of the first things they did was send a one-page letter, signed by the entire leadership team, to every employee's home. In it, they publicly committed to six things: (1) listening to one another and to all employees, (2) supporting one another and all employees, (3) challenging the status quo, (4) accepting accountability and responsibility for their personal actions, (5) communicating often and providing regular feedback, and (6) never forgetting that they were dedicated to making Menasha Packaging the most admired company in the industry. By itself, the letter might have come across as gimmicky. But together with the trips to every plant and the constant communication on strategic progress, the letter sent a powerful message that the team was serious about change.

In the following years, the leaders took things a step further to bring the strategy to life for people. They built a talent management system that connected corporate goals to divisional goals, plant goals, team goals, and finally individual goals. People can now see how their daily work is "rolling up" and driving company growth. That means that someone working a corrugating machine on a plant floor understands how the changes he is being asked to make are connected to increased revenue or decreased costs at the plant, division, and corporate levels. Everyone has a coherent context for his actions.

While Menasha's formal communication planning played a big part in its success over the last seven years, Waite will tell you that the most powerful communication tool couldn't be put into the plan. It was the leadership team's mindset.

"The glue that has made everything work was that we as senior leaders were open to genuinely listening to people," he said. "If we hadn't had that, everything else would have felt phony. To this day, we still walk the plant floors, shake hands, and hear what people have to say. Also, everyone has my direct phone line, which I answer myself. Any one of our 1,800 employees can call me. In fact, many of them do. They might not always like the answers I give them, but they know that I'm always going to listen to them and be honest."

Making an Insurance Company Nimble

Teams and organizations that are making big changes also have to be good at communicating at the project level, where the actual work gets done. In an increasingly technological world, fast and accurate communication is imperative for success. Small misunderstandings can mushroom into big problems if they are not caught and addressed early.

Of all the risks that insurance companies have to manage if they are to be successful, a rapidly changing business model has never been one of them until recently. For decades, the primary distribution channel for health, life, and disability insurance has been the same: brokers sell policies to groups (companies), which in turn provide them to members (employees). The model is effective because the products are complex and the broker can help the group and its members make sense of all the choices. Unfortunately, this model is also expensive and not transparent, making it ripe for disruptive competition.

"The slower-moving, broker-centered world is under attack," said Jill Dugan (names have been changed), VP of enterprise information technology at US Mutual, a top 10 U.S. insurer focused on life and disability insurance. "Look no further than Google's purchase of U.K.-based BeatThatQuote .com in 2011. It's a website that sells simpler products, like auto and home insurance, but that also sells the more complex products, like life and health insurance. The dynamics of how insurance is bought and sold are changing. We have to adapt or risk becoming irrelevant."

For US Mutual and other insurance companies, that means figuring out how to become more consumer-friendly. Products need to be less complex, easier to buy, easier to manage, and reasonably priced in order to succeed in multiple distribution channels. Dugan points out that many insurers understand this fact, but the trick is pulling it off.

"Insurance companies don't have the same nimble, rapid-execution cultures that the Googles of the world do," she said, pointing out a dynamic that has caused trouble in other industries, such as publishing and music. "Technology companies can brainstorm, build, and beta-test ideas in a matter of months. While we don't necessarily need to be that responsive, we do need to be more responsive than we are right now."

To that end, Dugan has spent the last several years honing US Mutual's execution capability with a specific focus on improving communication.

"Seven years ago, we got a big wake-up call," said Dugan. "After two years of development, we were gearing up to launch MutualManager, a high-profile system that would allow customers to manage their benefits online. Then, three months before going live, the team leading the project had to push back the launch date. They weren't asking for two more weeks or even two more months; they were asking for two more years. At the eleventh hour, they realized that they had the wrong functionality and would have to start over."

To an outsider, stories like this sound preposterous. How could an organization spend two years developing the wrong product without anyone raising a flag? To Dugan, who was brought in to figure out what went wrong and ensure that it didn't happen again, the answer was obvious: poor project management and poor communication discipline.

"When we dissected the problem, two big issues jumped out at us," Dugan said. "The first was that the people running the business were disengaged from the process. They wrote a set of requirements, shipped them to IT, and didn't have much meaningful interaction after that. The second issue was that there wasn't enough transparency. Without the expectation of regular business-IT interaction, there wasn't a forum to raise potential problems. Even if someone saw an issue, she didn't know how to bring it up, so she just swept it under the rug."

Two years later, MutualManager launched successfully, and Dugan had revamped project management practices across all group insurance projects.

One pivotal change that she's implemented is designating a business owner for every project. That person is responsible for ensuring that the project gets executed and meets business objectives. Citing a past problem of "orphan" projects that had no "parents" once they started to fail, Dugan now asks, "Whose job is in jeopardy if this project doesn't go well?"

If no one raises his hand or wants to take ownership, the project doesn't move forward.

"Many of the changes we've made have been around training business owners how to be business owners," Dugan explained. "For example, a director of large market underwriting didn't grow up in a project management environment and doesn't know what project execution means in terms of constant communication. We make it clear that if he's going to request significant resources for projects, he's got to take his oversight responsibilities seriously. That means that he has to get good at articulating his business problem, clarifying his expectations, managing progress along the way, actively participating in regular reporting meetings, and communicating any issues or changes to plans as things shift. While the business owner is partnered with a formal project manager who is managing the team and executing the work, it's made clear from the outset that the business owner is on the hook for delivering results."

The new project management practices are making a big difference. Teams are defining project requirements better, finding issues earlier, and delivering improved results for the business. Most important, there haven't been any big derailments like the first pass at MutualManager.

"In a way, we got lucky with MutualManager," Dugan said, explaining why she's been so focused on excellence in project execution. "We made that mistake at a time when it was merely expensive. In the future, a mistake like that could actually put us at a strategic disadvantage. Technology used to be behind the scenes, helping us run the business. More and more, technology *is* the business. As a result, we have to get good at seeing opportunities on the horizon and executing quickly and smartly in order to capitalize on them."

Creating a Compelling Case for a New Product

The previous two stories were examples of strengthening communication in environments where change already had momentum and many people were already involved. The following story demonstrates the importance of good communication when an idea or project is in its infancy and you might be the only one pushing it forward.

Products like toothpaste, mouthwash, and shampoo seem simple until you go behind the scenes and understand what it takes to bring them to market. Behind every successful consumer product is 5 to 10 years of research and development before it ever lands on a store shelf. And for every successful product, there are hundreds of good ideas that never get off the ground. Sometimes ideas don't make it because they're flawed. More often, it's a matter of limited resources. Developing new products takes a lot of time and money, which means that companies can make only so many bets. They have to go with the ideas that they feel have the best chance of winning in the market. Sometimes the decision to move forward comes down to how compelling a case R&D scientists can make about a new product.

In early 2004, Robert Glenn, then a principal scientist at Procter & Gamble (P&G), felt that he had a compelling case and a winning idea for a new product—a simple way to highlight hair at home.

Historically, home hair highlighting has not been a simple process. It requires mixing liquid chemicals together, covering floors and counters to avoid staining, and strategically applying the messy liquid in the right spots. The whole mixture must be used in one sitting, since it doesn't keep. At best, the process takes a long time; at worst, it can turn into a complete mess. After months of studying these challenges, Glenn felt that he had a solution that would make highlighting at home both easier and more effective.

The first key was turning the liquid into a solid form so that it wouldn't spill. Wanting to be thorough in his research, he visited several R&D teams around P&G to inform his thinking on this topic. They included Crest Whitestrips to understand how dentist-quality bleach was put onto small pieces of film; Cascade to understand how dish detergent was put into dissolvable pouches, and Swiffer floor cleaners to understand how these pads hold liquids so well. In all, he came up with 15 "solid form" ideas.

The second key was designing a better way to apply the chemicals. The right applicator would save consumers time, avoid messiness, and deliver a more even result. Trying to solve both liquid and application challenges, Glenn tested a variety of ideas and eventually came up with the idea for a clamshell-shaped device. P&G could preload the chemicals onto two different Swiffer-type pads, fasten them to two sides of the clamshell, and cover each until it was ready for use. Removing the protective covering and tapping the pads together would activate the colorant, skipping the need for messy mixing. Then the clamshell could be easily swiped through the hair to apply the highlights.

On several occasions Glenn presented his solid form and application ideas to R&D managers, including the clamshell. He was sure that the clamshell was a shoo-in for further exploration. Since he received great feedback on it from the managers, he figured that it would only be a matter of months before they started the development process. Surprising to Glenn, nothing happened.

For the next nine months, Glenn was pulled onto other projects that he was told were of higher priority. However, he kept the highlighting idea in the back of his mind, convinced that it had real commercial legs. Finally, in May 2005, frustrated that the idea hadn't gone anywhere yet, he decided to build it himself. Using barbecue tongs, cardboard, Velcro, Swiffer-type pads, and plastic wrap, he created a functional prototype of the highlighting product within a few days.

Next, Glenn invited some of the same R&D managers into the lab and handed one of them the barbecue tongs. He asked one of the managers to remove the plastic wrap, tap the tongs together to activate the colorant chemistry, and highlight a mannequin's hair just like someone might do at home. The result was a fast application, with no mess and nearly salon-quality highlights. The managers were impressed and decided to move forward with the idea. Seven years later, a version of the product is on the market as Clairol Perfect Lights.

Now a research fellow at P&G, Glenn shares the lessons he learned from that experience with other scientists in the company. "Communication doesn't happen when you share information with others; it happens when they understand the implications of the information. That's what the prototype helped do. It brought the concept to life so that people could really understand it. In retrospect, I realize that my initial presentations in 2004 didn't do that. My thinking was all over the place. I was sharing so many ideas that no one knew which ones to take seriously. The clamshell didn't stand out, even though all the same details were there and it was by far the best idea.

"The experience also showed me how often good ideas die because of poor communication. It's easy for someone on the technical side of our business to think that communication isn't a core part of her job because her expertise is the science. But great science won't get anywhere without great communication."

IDEAS AND TOOLS FOR ACTION

There are many ideas and tools that can strengthen communication. Here are five that I've found most helpful to clients in a variety of settings. They can all be scaled up or down depending on your needs.

Clarify the Information You Need to Communicate

A common complaint in organizations is that people don't feel that they're "in the loop" on important decisions, strategies, and paths forward. A big part of the problem is that leaders aren't clear on what they should be communicating. Table 14.1 shows eight types of information that it is important to share in times of significant change or risk taking. While you might not share them all at once, or with all audiences, taking the time to reflect and "unpack" your thinking on each puts you in a better position to communicate them effectively.

TABLE 14.1

Key Piece of Information	Description	Example	Common Problems in Communicating
1. Situation	The facts of the situation you're facing; the reason why the communication is important in the first place.	*Our growth in XX division has stalled. The market is getting tougher and tougher as business is being shipped overseas and price pressures are squeezing our margins.*	*Never gets shared.* The situation, insights, and implications are the backdrop for why action is being taken on a particular issue. Leaders often don't share this information because they erroneously assume that the information is obvious to everyone already. However, that's rarely the case. Laying out the information explicitly helps get everyone on the same page.
2. Insights	What you've learned over the past weeks or months as you've considered or researched the situation.	*We have really strong relationships with food companies that need high-value solutions that they can't get overseas and that are willing to pay a premium for service.*	
3. Implications	Your interpretation of what the situation and the insights gleaned mean for the road ahead.	*It would be smart to retool our operation to focus squarely on delivering solutions for food companies, where we're uniquely qualified to win. That means we'll have to cut out other lower-margin businesses.*	

TABLE 14.1 (*Continued*)

Key Piece of Information	Description	Example	Common Problems in Communicating
4. Vision (given the implications)	What you see on the horizon as the implications play themselves out over the coming years.	*We will be seen as a creative leader in delivering solutions to food companies. By having a niche focus, we'll be able to anticipate and proactively address customer needs faster than competitors.*	*Too vague and/or not compelling.* A compelling vision and strategy have to be at once inspiring and specific. People need to understand where they're headed at a high level and specifically how they will get there.
5. Strategies	What you understand will have to happen to realize the vision.	*We'll need to build stronger creative and marketing services expertise, retrain our current sales staff, and hire additional sales staff with knowledge of the food industry.*	
6. WIIFY (what's in it for you)	What people will gain personally. Powerful communication makes a convincing case for how individuals will benefit from the changes described.	*These changes are going to help us survive as a company. But it's more than that. You'll be able to feel like part of a winning team again. You'll deliver high value and creative solutions for customers, learning a lot in the process. It will be tough, but it will also be fun.*	*Isn't explicit enough.* WIIFY, WRFY, and next steps clearly define how a large effort translates to each individual. If people can't see the road right in front of them and the benefits of their effort, the message is unlikely to engage their hearts and minds.

(Continued)

TABLE 14.1 (*Continued*)

Key Piece of Information	Description	Example	Common Problems in Communicating
7. WRFY (what's required from you)	Being explicit about what will be required from people helps get them focused on what they need to do.	*This change is going to take a lot of effort. The hours will be long at times. At every turn, we're going to need your commitment and honest feedback in order to get better.*	Isn't explicit enough. WIIFY, WRFY, and next steps clearly define how a large effort translates to each individual. If people can't see the road right in front of them and the benefits of their effort, the message is unlikely to engage their hearts and minds.
8. Next steps	What people can expect in the coming weeks or months	*In the coming month, we'll be sharing a more detailed description of the strategy with you. In the meantime, a pilot team is already working on solutions for a few customers, and we should have results from those projects to share this month.*	

The example in Table 14.1 is for a large organizational change, but the framework can be used to communicate anything. For instance, if you've come up with a new idea that you want to share with the managers above you, you can go through the same type of unpacking process. Ask yourself: "What's the situation that led me to think this is a good idea? What insights did I have? What are the implications of those insights? What are my vision and strategy for executing it? What's in it for the managers if they support the idea? What's required of them to support the idea? If I get approval, what are my next steps?" I've even had clients use the framework as the outline for a business plan.

Build and Execute a Communication Plan

Once you know what information you need to communicate, you have to plan to communicate it. The details and complexity of a communication plan vary widely depending on needs. Factors that should be considered are what you're trying to communicate, how technical it is, how big the impact might be, and how large the audience is. Communication surrounding a process change that involves 50 people is very different from communication surrounding a culture change that involves 50,000 people. For the former, I've seen simple communication plans that are a few bullet points on a single sheet. For the latter, I've seen detailed spreadsheets that are thousands of lines long. However, there are a few common elements that all good communication plans share.

▶ *Impact analysis.* Who's going to be affected by the changes you're making? Think about the different divisions and different levels. Global companies need to consider multiple geographies. If there's a wide variety within your audience, different communication strategies may be required to ensure that each subset receives relevant information.

▶ *Messaging calendar.* Careful consideration should be given to how messages are sequenced and delivered. Perhaps they can all be delivered at once, or maybe they should be spread out over time. If there are specific dates when you expect to deliver results, make a note of them as well as other major events that are planned. As you review these points, it's helpful to place the communications on a calendar so that everyone can see them.

▶ *Messaging development.* Taking the time to develop messaging is key to any communication plan. You should allow for this in your messaging calendar as well. You may need to coordinate with your internal communications leader or solicit help from someone outside the organization to write and/or structure your communication. Think about who's going to approve the messaging to ensure that the themes and the language are consistent. This becomes particularly important with more complex communication vehicles like video.

▶ *A variety of communication vehicles.* How will you get your messages across? Town halls, small group meetings, e-mails, newsletters, and videos are all useful modes of communication. Delivering a consistent message across a variety of vehicles is most effective because different people pay attention to and respond better to different vehicles.

▶ *Opportunity for two-way communication.* The most important thing to remember about communication is making sure that it goes both ways. Getting feedback on the changes you're making will ensure that people feel that they are part of the process, which in turn makes them more likely to support your efforts. You can use formal methods, like surveys, or informal methods, like an open-door policy. There might be opportunities during regular staff meetings or one-on-one sessions. Be creative and capitalize on all the opportunities available.

Hold Regular, Useful Check-In Meetings

While most teams have check-in meetings, usually these meetings are only marginally effective. To make your check-ins more useful, I recommend these guidelines:

1. *Make the meetings regular.* Don't rely on ad hoc check-in meetings. They end up not happening often enough, and no one is really prepared to make them useful. Put regular meetings on the calendar, and prioritize the time in your weekly or monthly schedule.

2. *Pick the right things to talk about.* This is deceptively difficult for many teams to do. I've sat through executive team meetings in which 25 percent of the meeting was taken up discussing the flushing mechanism on the office toilets— clearly important, but something that could have been delegated. While this is an extreme example, things of this

sort happen all the time in meetings. To make the meetings useful, pick the top one to three things your team must focus on, send an agenda in advance (the decision brief tool in Chapter 8 is great for this), and be ruthless about not getting derailed.

3. *Stick to clear time boundaries.* Start on time. Allot time for each conversation so that nothing important gets missed. End on time. The better a team is at respecting time boundaries, the more effective its meetings are. People know that they'll get in, take care of business, and get out.

4. *Be crystal clear about the next action steps.* If everyone in the room isn't clear on what has to be done, by when, and by whom, there's little chance that it will get done. Put actions in writing (a simple e-mail usually suffices).

Leave Time for Informal Chats

Along with the formal planning and structures just discussed, make sure you're leaving opportunities to have informal conversations with people. It might be lunches, drinks, or just stopping them in the hall for 10 minutes. Much good information can be gleaned from the informal chats you can have between the big things you have to get done.

One leader I know, who's particularly busy, schedules regular time to sit down with colleagues without any agenda. He uses the opportunity to learn more about what they're working on, struggling with, or succeeding at, and he shares the same with them.

How Do You Know if You're Communicating Effectively?

Ask others. Don't rely on your own assessment. Communication doesn't occur when you speak. It occurs when people understand you. Speaking is only the tip of the iceberg. Just because others hear your words doesn't necessarily mean that they understand the thinking behind them. As a result, they can easily misconstrue what you say, even when you think you're being very clear. This is at the heart of the communication blind spot.

Here are several clarifying questions that will force you and others to make your thinking explicit and ensure that you're on the same page.

After You've Said Something

1. How does my thinking differ from yours?
2. What parts of my thinking aren't clear?
3. What do you see as the biggest challenges to my approach?
4. How would you improve on my ideas?

After You've Listened to Someone Else

1. Here's what I'm hearing. Is that correct?
2. I don't know how that would look. Can you give me an example?
3. I'm not sure of the best first step. What are your thoughts?
4. I understand the strengths of your approach. What do you see as its drawbacks?

Chapter 14 Summary

▶ Communication breakdowns are a reality of human interaction. In fact, they happen so often and so quickly that it's best to start with the assumption that they're going to happen at some point and plan accordingly.

▶ The most common reason that communication breaks down is the communication blind spot. As soon as something becomes clear to us, we have a tendency to think that it's just as clear to everyone else, too, so we don't put much time into communicating about it.

▶ A place where communication blind spots commonly occur is in communicating large strategic changes across an organization. As the Menasha case demonstrated, avoiding communication breakdowns in these scenarios requires thorough planning.

► Another place where communication blind spots occur is in project execution. US Mutual has been able to remove significant risk from its business by structuring project management more effectively, with a specific emphasis on strong communication throughout.

► When an idea is in its infancy, like Glenn's new product at P&G, it requires laser-sharp focus and compelling communication to get it out of the gate. Good ideas by themselves usually go nowhere.

CHAPTER FIFTEEN

Have the Tough Conversations

Lack of candor blocks smart ideas, fast action, and good people contributing all the stuff they've got. It's a killer.

—JACK WELCH, *Winning*

Chapter 14 points out that a common reason that communication breaks down is the *communication blind spot.* When we're moving quickly, we take our perspective for granted. We fail to realize that we see things that others don't see or have information that others don't have, so we don't communicate those things.

A second, more insidious reason that communication breaks down is *communication avoidance.* Unlike the blind spot, avoidance is intentional. We are aware that something is an issue, yet we don't bring it up. We might be afraid of how someone will react, or believe that we don't have the skills to have the conversation, or worry that having the conversation is going to take too much time and energy. We think it's smarter just to avoid the conversation altogether.

While there are good reasons to avoid tough conversations, in risk-taking scenarios, avoiding them can become a big problem. Trust decreases, errors go undetected, and efforts splinter, adding more risk to an already risky situation. I've found that it's next to impossible to do something big if you're not being straight with the people around you.

Let's look at two examples of how individuals and teams approached tough conversations effectively in the midst of uncertainty, rooting out problems, aligning efforts, and strengthening relationships.

Putting What's at Stake on the Table

Five years ago, if you had asked Mark Lynch, CEO of LifeScience (names have been changed), if his team was good at having tough conversations, he would have said unequivocally yes. With his company on the verge of bringing a groundbreaking new surgical tissue to market, he would have argued that too much was on the line and things were moving too fast to withstand people hiding things or not being totally honest. He prided himself on the fact that he called things the way he saw them, and he expected others to do the same.

The problem, however, was that Lynch was so forceful in his delivery that others rarely found room to engage in the same degree of candor. Lynch presented his ideas as foregone conclusions, driving his perspective forward, but rarely asking for others' viewpoints. The net effect was frequent one-way conversations that produced resentment, rather than deeper understanding. While Lynch knew the importance of tough conversations, he and his team were far from good at having them.

Susan McAndrew, a consultant who helped LifeScience senior management improve its team effectiveness during this critical time, explained what she saw as the heart of the issue. "People weren't having the real conversations. Lynch's approach was getting in the way of healthy dialogue. No one wanted to bring up potentially contentious or thorny issues for fear of being immediately shot down or publicly humiliated. However, it wasn't just Lynch that was at fault; the rest of Lynch's team also had a hand in the dynamic. They weren't picking spots where they could push back and share their thinking when it really mattered. The whole team's interactions had turned into a vicious cycle."

The wake-up call came in early 2007, when a significant product development challenge threatened LifeScience's meticulously calculated timeline. Several senior leaders had known about the issue for weeks but hadn't brought it to the team for a broader conversation. Having witnessed Lynch's harsh reactions in the past, they didn't want to raise the issue unprepared, so they were taking the time to gather extensive data, arming themselves for the onslaught. In the intervening weeks, it turned out that another member of the team could have provided helpful guidance that would have accelerated their ability to address the issue at a time when every day counted. When Lynch learned of these events, he nearly blew a gasket.

"Lynch talked to me privately to voice his frustration," McAndrew recalled. "He felt he was doing everything possible to foster open conversations, and yet more and more stuff wasn't being discussed. He couldn't figure out what to do differently because he didn't see his role in the problem."

As is often the case, the breakdown was a blessing in disguise. It provided Lynch and his team with a prime opportunity to get the real conversations and irritations out on the table.

In the ensuing months, McAndrew facilitated a series of team and small group sessions designed to bring these concerns to the surface. In those meetings, Lynch shared that he didn't think the team felt the same level of urgency that he did. From his perspective, the product under development was the game-changing future of their business. They were in a do-or-die situation, and he didn't feel that others appreciated how high the stakes really were. He admitted that the frustration and anger that people perceived from him came from his fear of failing at this crucial endeavor. The innovative product was complex, development costs were significant, and regulatory hurdles were everywhere. Lynch was afraid that the company might get beaten to market or, worse yet, not even make it to market and become obsolete.

On the flip side, several team members were upset about not being heard. Some said that they weren't sure how to bring up issues without invoking Lynch's wrath. Others felt that they *had* raised issues, but that Lynch hadn't been receptive to feedback. They said he didn't encourage open discussion of information and admitted that they'd gotten increasingly more selective about what they shared with him.

From the outside, these exchanges might sound like one big finger-pointing exercise, but they ended up being just the opposite.

"The conversations were an opportunity for each member of the group to recognize how he was contributing to problems by not discussing what was really on his mind," McAndrew said. "By the end of the meetings, each team member had committed to finding ways to raise issues more quickly and effectively in the future."

For example, Lynch and the head of marketing, Linda Bell, had a particularly rocky relationship. Yet it was also one of the most important relationships to the success of the new product. Lynch and Bell decided to have regular biweekly meetings to review progress on top priorities. Knowing that their conversations were inclined to derail, they agreed to check in at the end of their meetings using a simple question: "With regard to our relationship and the topic we just discussed, is there anything between us that I'm not bringing up?"

"They actually started to guess when the other might have an issue, which brought a little humor to their relationship," said McAndrew. "I can't say that they didn't have challenges going forward, but I can tell you that the regular, straightforward discussions helped them tackle some big issues that would have gotten in the way of the rapid execution needed to get their new product to market."

Managing Trust (in Addition to Building It)

At iShares, the ETF company introduced in Chapter 9, rapid execution was just as important as it was at LifeSciences. To iShares, it all came down to managing trust.

You may remember that in March 2000, only two months away from one of the largest and most complex investment fund launches in the history of the industry, CEO Lee Kranefuss pulled his 14-member leadership team off site for three days to discuss their interpersonal dynamics. While the people on his team thought he was crazy, Kranefuss saw the offsite as crucial. He knew that, as rough as things were during the launch phase, the road ahead was only going to get rougher. If the team didn't start addressing its relationship issues immediately, there might not be a future for the company.

"The March 2000 meeting opened some powerful conversations," said Tom Miller, a consultant and advisor who worked with the iShares management team during and after the launch. "There's no doubt that without that meeting, iShares would have significantly increased its risk of failure going into the launch. Team members uncovered and addressed issues that were undermining their relationships. And they began building a strong foundation of trust. However, that was only the beginning. In the months and years that followed, the people on the leadership team got faster at addressing sticky issues. They got better at *managing* the trust in their relationships, which was a key to their success."

When it comes to creating high-performing teams for the long term, Miller distinguishes *building* trust from *managing* trust. Building trust is the process of clearing up issues that prevent strong relationships. Managing trust is the process of keeping relationships strong as new issues arise. Miller uses the analogy of building and managing a house. The work isn't over once the house is built. It also has to be managed and maintained, or else it breaks down.

For iShares, managing trust meant bringing issues to the surface and addressing them in as close to real time as possible. Keenly aware of how important it was to set the tone at the top, Kranefuss was diligent about doing this. While the conversations were challenging at times, they kept the team focused on the task at hand, not on potential interpersonal issues. Soon the rest of the team followed suit and it became culturally unacceptable to keep interpersonal problems hidden.

Miller likened the mindset concerning trust at iShares to the working capital in a business. "Every business leader knows that no matter what assets you have on your balance sheet, you can't run a business without working capital. To iShares, trust became like *emotional* working capital. The people on the team saw it as a lifeline of their business. Without it, they couldn't operate. People would talk about it, acknowledge when it felt low, and take action to restore it."

Miller also helped the team distinguish between elements of trust so that they could be more accurate about what was causing breaches. Low trust didn't necessarily mean that one member was questioning another's motives; this was rarely a problem on this team. A more likely culprit was one member questioning another's process for accomplishing something. In these cases, trust in the person's *approach* was low, not trust in the person *herself*. However, if the issue went unaddressed for too long, it would translate into low trust in the person as well. That's exactly what the team didn't want and what made timely conversations so important.

The benefits of continually managing trust showed up not only in better relationships, but also in accelerated decision making at critical moments. J. Parsons, head of sales, pointed to a specific example of this right before the launch.

The team members realized that they hadn't accounted for a certain fee that would have a material impact on many of their planning assumptions and financial projections. All 14 members of the team dropped what they were doing and gathered in their "war room" to discuss how to address the potentially derailing issue.

"The miss was a big deal," Parsons made clear. "In every other organization I'd ever worked for, 14 managers would have spent hours, if not days, debating how to move forward. But with that team, because of the implicit trust we felt, within 10 minutes we made the decision to hand it off to the three people in the room who were best able to deal with it. The rest of us went back to what we needed to focus on to ensure an on-time launch. We knew that those three people would navigate the issue effectively, come to the right decision, and take care of it. And that's exactly what they did. No one ever second-guessed their decision. We just kept moving forward."

Parsons shared another story that's the ultimate testament to what this tight-knit iShares team was able to accomplish. By the summer of 2001, a year after launch, iShares had met or exceeded all its goals to that point, surprising nearly everyone. Parsons, Kranefuss, and a few other senior team members were sitting in a bar in New York City celebrating their success when Parsons recalls Kranefuss saying, "If I knew a year ago all of the things I know about this product now, I probably wouldn't have launched."

"The rest of us were floored," Parsons remembers. "That was a pretty strong statement coming from Lee, a guy who had just led one of the most successful fund launches ever. Here he is saying that if he had known how unbelievably difficult the journey was going to be, he probably wouldn't have undertaken it. It made me appreciate the magnitude of what we'd pulled off. It also made me appreciate what kind of team we had to be in order to do it. We didn't have to love one another or even like one another all the time, but we did have to support, respect, and trust one another. And the only way we could do that was by being completely honest with one another."

IDEAS AND TOOLS FOR ACTION

Having tough conversations is a lot like going to the gym. If you've never done it, you won't be that good at it at first, and it probably will hurt. But if you keep going, with time you'll get better, you'll build your muscles for it, and it will ultimately hurt much less.

The tools that follow will help you identify, prioritize, plan for, and have tough conversations. These are some of the most effective concepts I have used through the years. You can find additional resources for tough conversations in the notes at the back of the book.[1]

Be Clear About What You're Thinking and Feeling, but Not Saying

More than 30 years ago, Chris Argyris, the former Harvard Business School professor introduced in Chapter 12, and his colleague Donald Schon developed an incredibly simple, yet ingenious tool to help people understand what conversations they might be avoiding in a given situation. They call it the left-hand column exercise.[2] Doing this exercise is helpful any time you feel stuck regarding a particular issue with another person or group of people.

Left-Hand Column Exercise

1. Think of a particularly frustrating interaction you've had with the person or people in question.
2. Draw a line down the center of a sheet of paper.
3. In the right-hand column, to the best of your ability, reconstruct the actual dialogue in the interaction. Usually the more recent and more memorable the conversation, the better.
4. In the left-hand column, jot down what you were thinking and/or feeling at the moment that each thing was being said.
5. Review both columns, looking for differences between what you were thinking and feeling and what you and the other person or people were actually saying.
6. Identify areas where you think it's important to share the contents of your left-hand column with the other person or people.

Table 15.1 shows what the left-hand column exercise might look like in a real situation. Ryan, a marketing manager at a software firm, is preparing materials for the firm's channel partners to use in an upcoming promotion. Steve, his VP, wants to review them with the broader sales and marketing team before signing off. Ryan feels that he's already reviewed them to an appropriate degree and that Steve doesn't trust him. However, Ryan struggles to say anything about that fact.

TABLE 15.1

Left-Hand Column: What Ryan Was *Thinking* and/or Feeling	Right-Hand Column: What Steve and Ryan *Actually* Said
Since that mistake I made four years ago, Steve still doesn't trust my ability to get even the smallest document vetted and approved by the team. But he'll never say anything directly about my work product.	*Steve:* Your marketing materials look good. Let's get the team together to discuss them to see where others might have some thoughts or ideas to tighten them up.
I already know that the materials are directionally good and that the channel managers like them because I sat down with each of them to review the materials in detail.	*Ryan:* OK. I hope these look directionally good to you. I want to make sure whatever we end up using supports all the channels effectively.
I really don't think this is an efficient use of the team's time. The more we call everyone together to talk about this level of detail, the less effective our meetings become.	*Steve:* Yeah, I think they look good. It just occurred to me that we could all be coordinating on this stuff more effectively. There are probably ways the team could help.
I really wish Steve would engage more in the early stages of material development if he wants to engage at all, not after the materials are already in final draft. I tried to get two meetings on his calendar three months ago, but he canceled both of them.	*Ryan:* Just so you know, I sat down with each member in advance of sending you the materials and incorporated their feedback. Steve: I know. I just think ideas percolate better when everyone is together in a room.
This fire drill is going to delay the launch of these materials and screw up my planning for the next month. I wish I could bring that up with Steve.	*Ryan:* OK. I'll have 10 copies printed up for a meeting in the next week.

Reading through the conversation between Ryan and Steve, and looking at Ryan's corresponding left-hand column, you might find that you're empathizing more with one person or the other. Perhaps you're thinking that Steve needs to cut Ryan some slack. Or, conversely, you might be thinking that Steve is probably making a good point, as Ryan has proved untrustworthy in the past. There's certainly more to the story than we know. While only

Ryan's left-hand column is included, you can imagine Steve's as well.

The important takeaway is not that Ryan and Steve should bring up everything that's in their left-hand columns. Rather, it's a realization that the more they keep their thoughts and feelings hidden from each other, the less powerful their relationship will be and the more risk they will incur as they plan and execute their work. It's the same for all of us. We each have to be aware of what's in our left-hand column and find ways to share important thoughts.

Prioritize Your Tough Conversations

Whether it's by identifying the thoughts in your left-hand column or by some other means, you can become aware of a variety of tough conversations that you could be having. The trouble is, you can't have all of them or you'd never get anything done. You'd also probably go crazy if you tried. You have to pick your battles.

To determine whether or not you should have a particular tough conversation, I recommend using two questions, represented in the 2 × 2 matrix in Figure 15.1.

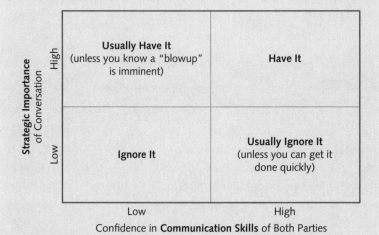

FIGURE 15.1   SHOULD I HAVE THIS TOUGH CONVERSATION?

First, *how strategically important is the issue, and why?* If it's strategically important, you should usually figure out a way to have the conversation, no matter how tough it is. If it's not strategically important, you should usually ignore it, even if you feel you're "right" or you want to make a point.

Second, *how confident am I in my skill and the other party's skill in engaging in the conversation?* If you have high confidence in both of your skills and it's strategically important, have the conversation. If you have low confidence in both of your skills and it's *not* strategically important, ignore the conversation. You can see these choices in Figure 15.1 in the upper right and lower left boxes, respectively.

The "grayer" choices are found in the upper left and lower right boxes, with the trickier being the upper left box: high strategic importance and low confidence in someone's skills (yours, the other party's, or both). This is the box that causes the most problems in organizations because it often goes unaddressed. While I've labeled the conversations in this box as "Usually Have It," many people treat them as "Usually Ignore It." For obvious reasons, that leads to trouble when you're taking risks and trying to make important changes.

My recommendation is that you put the upper left conversations at the top of your priority list and find ways to have them, even though they're the toughest. The next two tools can help in raising "upper left" concerns more effectively.

Plan the Tough Conversation Before You Have It

Some people are better than others at having tough conversations. Regardless, everyone can improve at having them. One thing I recommend to anyone, whether he considers himself highly skilled at communicating or not, is to plan a tough conversation before having it. Doing so pulls you out of your own narrow viewpoint to let you see the situation from a variety of perspectives.

The following eight questions take about 30 minutes to think about and are a great planning tool. They're worded in the past tense, but you can use them in the present as well, as you're actively going through a situation. Reflecting on them can put you in a much better place to succeed.

(These questions are adapted from *Difficult Conversations* by Doug Stone, Bruce Patton, and Sheila Heen.)

With Regard to Me

1. What's my story about what happened?
2. What was my intent in this situation?
3. How has the situation affected me?
4. How did I contribute to the situation?

With Regard to the Other Person or Party

5. What do I think the other person's story is about what happened?
6. What do I think was her intent in this situation?
7. How has the situation affected her?
8. How did she contribute to the situation?

The first four questions will help you understand your own thoughts and feelings about the situation, as well as where you might have been complicit in creating it. The second four will put you into the other person's shoes, which it is always smart to do before addressing a touchy subject.

Balance Advocacy and Inquiry when Having the Conversation

Related to the recommendation in Chapter 13 that you listen twice as much as you talk, making your tough conversations productive requires that you balance advocacy and inquiry.[3] Advocacy is stating your point of view, or what you see as a fact. Inquiry is asking questions to deepen your appreciation and understanding of another's point of view.

When you're in a tough conversation, your job is to share your reflections on Questions 1 to 4 from the planning exercise (advocacy). Simultaneously, your job is to ask questions that shed light on how accurate your guesses at the answers to Questions 5 to 8 were (inquiry). You'll usually find that you got some things right and some things wrong, opening important points for discussion.

Balancing advocacy and inquiry tends to create productive, honest conversations.

A Word About Trust

Trust is at the foundation of being able to have fast and useful tough conversations. In the iShares example earlier in the chapter, I mentioned that Tom Miller helped the team members distinguish between elements of trust so that they could accurately pinpoint breaches and focus restorative conversations on the right area(s).

Table 15.2 helps clarify what trust means. When you say, "I do or don't trust this person," you're dynamically assessing four elements of trust. Only one of these elements has to be low for trust to feel low. The questions next to each of the four elements are a good way to help you determine possible gaps in your trust with someone. They also show where you should focus if you need to rebuild or manage trust with someone.

TABLE 15.2

Element of Trust (Only one has to be low for trust to feel low)	Assessment Questions (The stronger the yes, the higher the trust)
Competence	Do I believe that this person has the requisite abilities for the task at hand?
Reliability	Can I trust this person to: ▶ Take the task seriously? ▶ Do what he said he'd do? ▶ Get the job done?
Motive	Am I clear on this person's motives? Do I trust her motives?
Openness/Quality of Communication	Do I feel that this person makes an effort to keep me "in the loop" on what he's doing? Do I feel that he is being open and honest with me?

Chapter 15 Summary

▶ In addition to the *communication blind spot* introduced in Chapter 14, *communication avoidance* is another reason that communication breaks down. Unlike the blind spot, avoidance is intentional, often making it tougher to address.

▶ The impact of communication avoidance in risk-taking scenarios is particularly problematic because it adds more risk to an already risky situation. Trust decreases, errors go undetected, and efforts splinter.

▶ The LifeSciences example pointed to the idea that not all tough conversations are productive tough conversations. Forcefully sharing your ideas without creating room for others to share theirs shuts down dialogue.

▶ The iShares example demonstrated the importance of both building and managing trust to create an environment that is conducive to having tough conversations.

▶ Getting better at having tough conversations takes energy. First efforts never feel good. However, with time and practice, these conversations hurt less, get faster, and serve as the foundation for sustainable success.

PART SIX

CREATE A
SMART-RISK
CULTURE

Supporting Smart Risk Taking

What gets measured gets managed.

—PETER DRUCKER

By this point in the book, it should be obvious that smart risk taking isn't a series of crazy bets and gutsy heroics. Rather, it's a thoughtful process of planning, experimenting, and learning that is designed to generate new ideas and drive growth more consistently. Like any challenging process, it needs to be supported in order to flourish.

First, supporting smart risk taking requires defining what it means in your organization, distinguishing smart risks from other risks, and getting things down to explicit expectations and behaviors that can be shared and discussed. You need to set the field of play, helping everyone understand what's "in bounds" and what's "out of bounds."

Next, smart risk taking, and especially smart failure, must be explicitly and consistently encouraged. Encouraging smart failure sends the message that more than results count; learning and generating new insights are just as important to the future of the company.

One place where companies are starting to get good at encouraging smart failures is in innovation programs. Following are two stories of organizations that have found productive ways to encourage and reward smart risk taking and smart failure, creating a smart-risk culture in the process.

Acknowledging Those Who Dare to Try

Ever since Jamsetji Tata built his first cotton mill in the 1870s, risk taking and innovation have been at the heart of Tata Group's growth. Today, the India-based concern is a multinational conglomerate, with more than 400,000 employees working in more than one hundred operating companies around the world. Market leaders in everything from steel and chemicals to telecommunications and energy, Tata Group relies heavily on risk taking and innovation to find its next big ideas.

In 2007, seeing new idea generation as a defining competitive advantage, Tata senior executives created the Tata Group Innovation Forum (TGIF), a collection of strategic innovation initiatives focused on strengthening thought leadership and knowledge sharing. TGIF also places a strong emphasis on celebrating and encouraging innovation so that employees feel supported in taking smart risks.

A big part of the celebration and encouragement for risk taking comes from Tata Innovista, an annual innovation award program. Comprising four award categories, Tata Innovista identifies and showcases the best innovation efforts of the past year. The categories are based on the ideas' position in the innovation pipeline, from initial concept to launch.

Leading Edge—Unproven Idea is early-stage ideas that haven't been developed yet. *Leading Edge—Proven Technology* is ideas that have been developed and tested, but not commercialized yet. *Promising Innovation* is ideas that have been launched successfully. And *Dare to Try* is ideas that have failed, yet were worthy endeavors.

Participation in Tata Innovista has jumped from 282 entries in 2008 to 2,852 in 2012. Part of the growth is the result of better communication about the program, but a bigger factor is increased understanding among employees that senior executives take it seriously. Ratan N. Tata, the company's CEO (retired in December 2012), personally hands out each of the 10 to 20 awards every year.

Employees are also clear that executives are taking the innovation *process* itself seriously, not just results. The Dare to Try award gives formal recognition to Tata's belief that smart failures are as critical to innovation as smart successes. The open acceptance of smart failures creates a different innovation culture at Tata from the one you find at most companies. The idea that you can be publicly congratulated by the CEO for failing intelligently sends a powerful message. Usually, people want to hide their failures, but at Tata, teams readily submit their failures to be judged by management (132 of them in 2011).

The Dare to Try award works because Tata's definition of a smart failure is very specific. Each Dare to Try submission is judged on four criteria: (1) How novel or unique was the attempted outcome? (2) What was the projected impact of the outcome (economic, social, and environmental)? (3) What risks were involved, and how well were they managed? (4) Is the team raring to go again? Each criterion is ranked on a five-point sliding scale that deems the failure as more or less favorable, giving people a clear idea of the variables that make risk taking smart at Tata (Table 16.1).[1]

Each box spells out clearly what outcomes earn what rankings, yet the matrix isn't too prescriptive, leaving room for interpretation and dialogue. The three other Innovista innovation awards have similar matrices, providing actionable risk-taking guidelines at all stages of innovation. Teams can use the frameworks as continual measuring sticks to understand where they are and aren't taking smart risks.

To give you an idea of what wins a Dare to Try award, there were two handed out in 2011. One was for a portable cardiac device that couldn't find traction in the market, but that indirectly resulted in new business with other clients and a new service model for India's healthcare system. Another award was for a jelly drink that didn't sell well in the United Kingdom, but that might hold possibilities for a new product category down the road. In both situations, Tata executives felt that, despite the failure, the benefits of the risk-taking process were significant and should be acknowledged.

TABLE 16.1 TATA INNOVISTA'S *DARE TO TRY* AWARD—EVALUATION CRITERIA

Favorably increasing scale →

Novelty or uniqueness of the attempted outcome (25%)	The outcome would have been unique to the company An old idea tweaked—very obvious given the situation (problem or opportunity)	The outcome would have been unique to the company or to Tata Group A new idea—somewhat obvious given the situation (problem or opportunity)	The outcome would have been unique to the industry A new idea—not obvious given the situation (problem or opportunity)	The outcome would have been unique to the country across industries. It has changed the rules of the game A new and bold idea—slight shift in the current paradigm/mental model	The outcome would have been unique to the world A new and audacious idea—significant shift in the current paradigm/mental model
Projected impact of the outcome (economic, social, and environmental) (25%)	The outcome would have had: One-time marginal impact on the company in the metrics related to economic, social, or environmental issues	The outcome would have had: One-time substantial impact on the company in the metrics related to economic, social, or environmental issues Limited impact on target customer(s) Limited impact (influence) on the industry	The outcome would have had: Substantial impact on metrics related to economic, social, or environmental issues Moderate impact on target customer(s) Moderate impact (influence) on the industry	The outcome would have had: Substantial medium-term impact on metrics related to economic, social, or environmental issues Considerable impact on target customer(s) Considerable impact (influence) on the industry(ies)	The outcome would have had: Substantial long-term impact on metrics related to economic, social, or environmental issues Very substantial impact on target customer(s) Substantial impact (influence) on several industries

Risks involved (25%)	There was no risk involved in the project	There was very little risk involved	There was some risk involved, and the steps taken to derisk to derisk were inadequate	There was a good amount of risk, and the team took adequate steps to derisk	The project was very risky, and the team focused on and succeeded in derisking it to the extent possible
Raring to go again (25%)	The team was disheartened The management penalized the team members	The team members are not sure if they would be able to get/take up similar assignments in future Management has penalized a few members selectively	The team has learned from its mistakes and is eager to take up the next assignment Management has given the team new, challenging assignments, although not related to the innovation project	The organization has learned from the mistake. The team has done extensive research on the reasons for failure Management has communicated the failure to the relevant parts of the organization in a positive note	The organization has deployed the learnings in the form of suitable processes Management has appreciated the efforts and risk taken by the team members. The team has been given more resources and knowledge to carry out further or new work

At an Innovista event a few years ago, Tata senior executive and TGIF head R. Gopalakrishnan summarized the role of TGIF as fourfold:

- Create an atmosphere in which passion can grow.
- Remove barriers that have been inadvertently created.
- Bring people together.
- Encourage people.

On this last point, he emphasizes that a key to encouragement is recognizing innovations that both worked and did not work. Celebrating the passion, commitment, and attempts made, successful or not, leads to a culture that enthusiastically supports innovation.

Increasing Entrepreneurship in Corporate IT

Initiatives to support innovation and risk taking can also happen at department and group levels without being mandated by C-suite executives.

You don't normally think of people who manage things like phone systems and data centers as being entrepreneurial. David Richter, VP of ITS infrastructure solutions at consumer products company Kimberly-Clark (K-C), sees that as a problem. Responsible for 260 professionals that support all IT hardware across the globe for K-C, Richter believes that developing an entrepreneurial approach to corporate IT is pivotal to his team's ability to stay on top of rapidly changing technology.

"Things move too fast for me or my managers to see all the innovative opportunities in the market," Richter said. "And frankly, we're just not smart enough to do it even if we had the time. We need everyone in the group thinking like entrepreneurs, looking for new innovations, and taking smart risks in order to continuously improve."

Of course, that's easier said than done. A couple of years ago, as he first thought about addressing the issue, Richter knew that the people in his group were sharp, creative thinkers, but he also knew that too much process and fear of failure would block their ideas. He was looking for a way to open up their thinking and give them room to experiment.

His solution, inspired by his experience at four start-ups prior to K-C, was to invite venture capital– (VC-) style pitches from anyone in his group for any changes she wanted to make. If someone had an idea for a new machine, a new method, or a new process, she could schedule time on his calendar to try to sell it to him.

A year later, the VC approach has become a big hit. Here's how it works. An individual or team puts together a one-sheet description of the idea, clarifying the benefits to K-C, the scope of the initial test, and the resources needed. The person or team members pitch Richter for 30 minutes or less, during which time he acts as both a funder and a coach, helping the people frame their ideas more tightly. If they have a fundable idea, he provides the requested money for a phase 1 test, usually less than three months and a couple of thousand dollars (sometimes the ideas take no money at all). If the test is successful, the department either does a broader test or puts the idea into production immediately.[2]

"My expectation going in was that a large majority of the efforts would fail, much like many VC-backed concepts," Richter said. "But I've been surprised that most of them have succeeded. It demonstrated to me that the team has a lot of great ideas that just need to be brought to life."

Richter is quick to point out that he doesn't measure success on business outcomes alone, but also by what was learned. He publishes the results of every funded idea, whether it succeeds or fails, on an internal website, and also sends an e-mail around to his group and sometimes to others at K-C, detailing takeaways.

"That changed people's perceptions about taking risks," explained Richter. "When everyone in my group saw that we were making a big deal about learning from failure and stressing how the lessons would help us down the road, people felt freer to suggest more ideas. They also felt motivated and encouraged by the public recognition they'd get, no matter what the outcome, if the idea was pursued intelligently."

Like any other entrepreneur, people who get an idea funded by Richter aren't given a process for making the idea work. They have to figure it out on their own. They also have to pursue it in addition to their "day jobs"; they don't get special time carved out for these projects. If they need help from other people in the organization, it's the same. They have to convince those people to donate their time. The result is that people think like owners of the business, weighing the pros and cons of every decision.

In one recent success, an employee created a mobile videoconferencing platform that could be placed in any room. Built and tested in one location, it's now ready to be rolled out companywide. In one recent failure, two employees tried to find a solution that would enable smartphones to dynamically switch from a network carrier to Wi-Fi for voice calls, which would have saved K-C hundreds of thousands of dollars a year in roaming charges. Although the technology wasn't ready yet, the team now knows exactly what to look for when it does become ready.

When I commented to Richter that his VC concept seems so simple, he responded that it's simple by design. "We wanted to create the least amount of bureaucracy possible. As soon as people have to jump through a lot of hoops to do something, they stop doing it. For any new idea, an employee could literally pitch it and be working on it in a matter of days. And because we agree on the scope together, they know I'm going to support them no matter what the outcome. People are really having fun with it."

IDEAS AND TOOLS FOR ACTION

Define Smart Risks in Your Organization

Use the ideas throughout this book (or other ideas of your own) to define what a smart risk looks like in your organization. It can be more involved, like Tata's Dare to Try award, or simpler, like Richter's VC pitch. What's most important is that employees are clear about what's expected of them and under what circumstances failures are OK.

A simple example would be to use the "Is Your Risk Taking Smart?" assessment at the end of Chapter 3. Alternatively, you could create your own definition or checklist. Specific elements are less important than having your group aligned on an accepted approach.

Acknowledge Smart Failures the Same Way You Do Smart Successes

As both examples in this chapter demonstrate, there's a lot of value in acknowledging smart failures in public. Tata uses awards and Richter uses postings and e-mail announcements, both of which work well. Additionally, it's also helpful to acknowledge smart failures in performance management and feedback processes, both formally and informally.

Role-Model Smart Risk Taking

One of the best ways to support smart risk taking is to role-model the behaviors for others to see. That means taking the time to co-create something worth fighting for with the rest of your team, predicting fail points together, and testing hypotheses in small ways before you really know what you're doing. It also means sharing smart failures with everyone around you so that they can get more comfortable doing the same.

There's a leadership maxim, *what you do speaks so loudly that people can't hear what you say.* That's never truer than when it comes to taking risks.

Chapter 16 Summary

- ▶ Smart risk taking, like any challenging process, has to be supported in order to flourish.
- ▶ Two keys to supporting smart risk taking are defining what a smart risk is and then encouraging smart risk taking, even when those risks end in smart failures.

▶ Encouraging smart failures sends an important message that more than results count.

▶ One way to support smart risk taking is through formal recognition programs such as Tata's. By clearly defining what smart innovation looks like, including smart failures, Tata sends a compelling message about what kind of behavior it expects.

▶ A simpler but also powerful concept is David Richter's VC idea at Kimberly-Clark. He's building a smart-risk culture by funding and supporting new ideas at the hypothesis stage and celebrating learning whether the ideas succeed or fail.

▶ One of the best ways to support smart risk taking is to role-model the behaviors yourself for others to see.

CHAPTER SEVENTEEN

The Virtuous Cycle of Taking Smart Risks

. . . the end of all our exploring
Will be to arrive where we started
And know the place for the first time.

—**T. S. ELIOT,** "Little Gidding V"

I hope this book has deepened your appreciation of risk taking as a set of skills that can be learned, practiced, and sharpened. While there's always a degree of art to taking risks—and some people are more naturally skilled at it than others—everyone can improve, finding smart ways to push outside her comfort zone.

Smart risk taking is about creating new things, understanding what you're made of, and feeling confident and alive. You lose these when you play it safe for too long, in essence losing the "life" in life. So you need to take risks. But even when you know that you need to take risks, fear can still stop you from doing it. It's only by being aware of what's at stake when you do *not* take risks—loss of growth, progress, and learning—that you find the right risks to take.

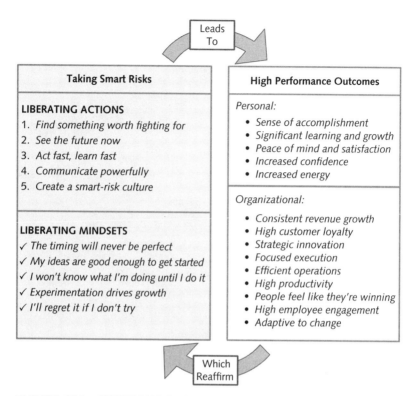

FIGURE 17.1 VIRTUOUS CYCLE OF TAKING SMART RISKS

Having a balanced focus on the costs and benefits of risk taking puts you in the smart-risk zone. There, liberating mindsets increase your confidence to take risks. In turn, these mindsets lead to liberating actions. Over time, the mindsets and actions strengthen each other, producing high performance outcomes at both individual and organizational levels. I call this the virtuous cycle of taking smart risks (see Figure 17.1). With every smart risk comes more learning, more confidence, and better results.

But you can produce positive outcomes only if you continue to take risks. If you idle in "neutral" too long, you end up in a different cycle, the vicious cycle of playing it safe (see Figure 17.2). Here you produce increasingly poor performance outcomes until you get stuck in a rut.

I share these two risk cycles to point out that there's no third option. There is no place where you can just stop risking

FIGURE 17.2   VICIOUS CYCLE OF PLAYING IT SAFE

and have everything remain in the status quo. Once you stop risking, you quickly stop growing. You stop producing results. You stop feeling alive.

Of course, everyone's risks look different. Some are big, some are small. Some are fast, some are slow. What's too easy for one person is frightening for another. You must decide on the risks that are appropriate for you. More important than the specific risks you choose is that you're continually stretching yourself.

In presenting the five components of smart risk taking, I've tried to share stories, ideas, and tools in small chunks so that they're easy to digest. At the same time, I know that no matter how information is laid out in a book, when you get to the last chapter, the sheer volume of what's been presented can feel muddled. So here are my CliffsNotes for key takeaways:

Find Something Worth Fighting For

▶ Carve time out of your schedule to stop and think about what you're willing to fight for. You must plan for it proactively because it is nearly impossible to do this type of thinking in the course of your normal daily routine. If it's helpful, do it with other people.

▶ Find a SWFF that's challenging, something that you can and want to be good at, and something that makes a positive contribution. This ensures that the SWFF will have staying power and be truly motivating.

▶ If you're clarifying a SWFF for your organization, ensure that it stirs emotion and inspires action. It should not feel like word-smithed corporate-speak. It should feel like something that everyone cares deeply about. It's helpful to engage a broad cross section of people for input to the SWFF.

See the Future Now

▶ Trust your instincts. The things you see and feel all around you are the most important data you can collect on the future. Never discount your own perspective. There's a good chance that you're the only one seeing things from your particular vantage point.

▶ Conversely, don't trust *only* your perspective. Get out of the office and spend time with other people, especially customers. Pieces of the future are strewn everywhere, and the more you explore, the more you will find.

▶ Make decisions. Give yourself time, but don't draw things out too long. Review data, talk things over with others, predict your fail points, and then decide on a course of action. Deciding builds energy on a team. Not deciding saps it.

Act Fast, Learn Fast

▶ Start before you know where to start. In the beginning of any endeavor, things are never very clear. Remember that the first hurdle is often the hardest, and that the actions needed to get out of the gate are often smaller than you realize.

▶ Fail fast, cheap, and small. Continually test hypotheses about what it will take to succeed. Learn from what you find, and then do more tests. Remember that the absence of failure isn't a positive sign. It's a sign that you're not taking enough chances.

▶ Learn from everything. Remember that you're at your weakest when you think you know all the answers. Make team learning opportunities (such as debriefings) simple and structured so that you can harvest helpful lessons quickly.

Communicate Powerfully

▶ Assume that your communication is bad. Even if it's good, assume that it will be bad soon. This is because no matter how effective we are at communicating, we all fall victim to the communication blind spot at times—thinking that something is clear to everyone else just because it's clear to us.

▶ Put regular communication structures in place to stay aligned during risk taking. Don't rely solely on ad hoc meetings or random conversations, which tend not to happen often enough to manage risks effectively.

▶ Have tough conversations when they come up. Make it an expectation that those around you will do the same. Doing so decreases risk in already risky situations and increases trust.

Create a Smart-Risk Culture

▶ Define the behaviors and expectations that demonstrate a smart risk in your organization so that people are clear about whether or not they're taking such risks—and if they're not taking them, what they need to change.

▶ Measure smart risks by a broader set of results than just project success. Measure learning generated and disseminated in the organization. Measure impact on future opportunities. Acknowledge smart failures that might have missed project goals but delivered value in other ways. Doing so sends a strong message about your commitment to risk taking.

Following the strategies in this book will make your risks smarter, increasing your confidence and decreasing your fear. While the advice can't guarantee success, it will definitely improve your chances of it.

As you consider the areas of your business or your life where you want to take more risks, ask yourself the proverbial question, "What have I got to lose?" More often than not, if you size up the risk honestly, you'll find that you've got more to lose by *not* taking it than by taking it.

In all the years I've been helping people push themselves and their organizations further, I've never once heard anyone say that he regretted taking a smart risk. When done intelligently, risk taking never leaves you empty-handed. Even in failure, the experience provides critical learning for the future.

The key is to start moving. Your path forward becomes clear once you're walking on it, not before. The risk-taking journey always brings challenges, but it also brings the strength and skill to deal with them. It always feels difficult, but it also feels meaningful and rewarding. And in the end, the journey always brings the same two realizations. You didn't have to be a hero to succeed; you just had to keep moving. And the greatest risk in life is never risking at all.

ABOUT THE AUTHOR

Doug Sundheim is a leadership and organizational consultant with over 20 years of experience in growing businesses and helping others do the same. He works with leaders and teams of Fortune 500 companies and entrepreneurial firms to help them maximize their effectiveness. His clients include Morgan Stanley, Harvard Management Company, The Chubb Corporation, Citigroup, University of Chicago, and Procter & Gamble among others.

Prior to his work in leadership and organizational consulting, Doug spent several years in the Internet strategy field and started a 100-person catering company. He holds a BS from Cornell University and an MA in Adult Learning and Leadership from Columbia University. He lives in Westchester, NY with his wife and two sons.

Doug regularly speaks, consults, and does workshops with leaders and teams. If you'd like more information about how he can help your organization, you can reach him at the information below.

Doug Sundheim
info@dougsundheim.com
(866) 245-2870

NOTES

Chapter 1 – "The Dangers of Playing It Safe"

1. Mihaly Csiksentmihalyi, *Flow: The Psychology of Optimal Experience* (New York: Harper Perennial Modern Classics, 2008) and Rollo May, *The Courage to Create* (New York: W. W. Norton & Company, 1994, originally published in 1959) are two excellent resources discussing the need for meaningful challenges in living a satisfying life. Maslow, cited in the next note is an excellent resource as well.

2. Abraham Maslow's well-known hierarchy of needs places physiological needs at the bottom, then moves up through safety, love and belonging, and esteem needs to self-actualization at the top. He first laid out this model in "A Theory of Human Motivation," *Psychological Review* 50, no. 4 (1943): 370–396. A free copy can be downloaded at http://psychclassics.yorku.ca/Maslow/motivation.htm.

   In 2010, Douglas Kenrick and colleagues offered a reformulation of Maslow's pyramid based on modern evolutionary theory. Their model splits components of self-actualization between two other categories and puts mating and parenting needs at the top. See Douglas T. Kenrick, Vladas Griskevicius, Stephen L. Neuberg, and Mark Schaller, "Renovating the Pyramid of Needs: Contemporary Extensions Build Upon Ancient Foundations," *Perspectives on Psychological Science* 5, no. 3 (2010): 292–314.

   In rebuttal, Christopher Peterson and Nansook Park question the dismissal of self-actualization, which, in their positive psychology research, they identify as a paramount human growth need. See "What Happened to

Self-Actualization? Commentary on Kenrick et al. (2010)," *Perspectives on Psychological Science* 5, no. 3 (2010): 320–322.

In his famous job attitude research in the 1950s and 1960s, psychologist Frederick Herzberg also found that growth and achievement were important factors. His studies revealed what came to be known as the two-factor theory (or motivator-hygiene theory).

Herzberg's data showed that extrinsic "hygiene" incentives such as pay, working conditions, and security (Maslow's lower-order needs) led to job dissatisfaction if expectations were not met, but weren't enough to motivate performance for long if they were met. On the other hand, intrinsic "motivator" factors such as achievement, recognition, and opportunities for growth (Maslow's higher-order needs) led to job satisfaction and people working harder for longer. The revelation of the study was that each set of factors worked independently of the other.

You can read the original research in Frederick Herzberg, Bernard Mausner, and Barbara Block Snyderman, *The Motivation to Work* (New York: John Wiley & Sons, 1959). Years later, Herzberg reprised his findings in what has become the most popular *Harvard Business Review* article, entitled "One More Time: How Do You Motivate Employees?" *Harvard Business Review* 65, no. 5 (September-October 1987): 109–120, http://hbr.org/2003/01/one-more-time-how-do-you-motivate-employees/ar/1.

Chapter 2 – "Shifting Your Perception of Risk—the Smart-Risk Zone"

1. Kahneman and Tversky's extensive body of groundbreaking research on heuristics and biases began in the 1970s. Kahneman's latest book, *Thinking, Fast and Slow* (New York: Farrar, Straus and Giroux, 2011) gives a rich accounting of their explorations of the machinery of the mind. Read about loss-aversion bias on pages 282–286.

The original article on loss aversion is Daniel Kahneman and Amos Tversky, "Process Theory: An Analysis of Decision Under Risk," *Econometrica* 47, no. 2 (1979): 263–291.

Chapter 4 – "What Are You Willing to Fight For?"

1. See Michael F. Steger's short review of the psychological literature on "Meaning in Life," *Oxford Handbook of Positive Psychology*, 2nd ed., eds. Shane J. Lopez and C. R. Snyder, chapter 64 (New York: Oxford University Press, 2009).
2. Viktor Frankl, *Man's Search for Meaning: An Introduction to Logotherapy* (New York: Washington Square Press, 1963).

Chapter 5 – "Finding the Fight in Your Organization"

1. The elements of a good SWFF are similar to the six principles that Chip Heath and Dan Heath lay out in *Made to Stick: Why Some Ideas Survive and Others Die* (New York: Random House, 2007). Sticky ideas tend to be simple, unexpected, concrete, credible, emotional, and provide inspirational stimulation through stories. If you're looking for a meaningful SWFF for your organization, the Heaths' book can help.
2. Robert McKee's quotation is from Bronwyn Fryer, "Storytelling That Moves People: A Conversation with Screenwriting Coach Robert McKee," *Harvard Business Review* 81, no. 6 (June 2003): 6, http://hbr.org/2003/06/storytelling-that-moves-people/ar/1. You can find Robert McKee's story methods, based on his popular seminars, in his book *Story: Substance, Structure, Style and the Principles of Screenwriting* (New York: Regan Books, 1997).

Chapter 6 – "The Future Is All Around You"

1. J.C.R. Licklider and Welden Clark, "Man-Computer Symbiosis," *(IRE Transactions on Human Factors in Electronics, Volume HFE-1, March 1960,)* accessed August 27, 2012 http://medg.lcs.mit.edu/people/psz/Licklider.html.
2. Scott Griffin, "Internet Pioneers: J.C.R. Licklider," accessed August 27, 2012 http://www.ibiblio.org/pioneers/licklider.html.
3. J.C.R. Licklider and Welden Clark, "On-Line Man-Computer Communication" (Spring Joint Computer Conference, National Press, Palo Alto, California, May 1962, vol. 21, pp. 113-128). accessed August 27, 2012: http://academic.googlecode.com/svn-history/r299/trunk/monografias_pessoais/cegsic_monografia/doc_tecnicos/046F1309d01.pdf.

4. J.C.R. Licklider and Robert W. Taylor, "The Computer as a Communication Device" (*Science and Technology*, no.76, Apr. 1968, pp. 21-31), accessed August 27, 2012: http://www .comunicazione.uniroma1.it/materiali/20.20.03_licklider-taylor .pdf.

5. Much of the background for the J.C.R. Licklider story can be found at: William Stewart, "Internet History—J.C.R. Licklider," http://livinginternet.com, accessed August 27, 2012: http://livinginternet.com/i/ii_licklider.htm.

Chapter 7 – "See the World Through Your Customers' Eyes"

1. Tom Connellan's book on exceptional customer experiences is *Inside the Magic Kingdom: Seven Keys to Disney's Success* (Ann Arbor, MI: Peak Performance Press, 1997). While it doesn't discuss the specific military example referred to in Chapter 7, it provides useful ideas for thinking about continual focus on customers.

Chapter 8 – "Stop, Think, Discuss, and Decide"

1. Psychologist and behavioral economist Dan Ariely, well known for his creative research, offers wise commentary on closing doors in "Keeping Doors Open: Why Options Distract Us from Our Main Objective," chapter 9 in *Predictably Irrational: The Hidden Forces That Shape Our Decisions*, revised and expanded edition (New York: Harper Perennial, 2010).

2. Ross D. E. MacPhee, curator of the Division of Vertebrate Zoology at the American Museum of Natural History, wrote a companion book for the "Race to the End of the Earth" exhibition. See *Race to the End: Amundsen, Scott, and the Attainment of the South Pole* (New York: Sterling Innovation, 2010).

3. Edward Larson's book is *An Empire of Ice: Scott, Shackleton, and the Heroic Age of Antarctic Science* (New Haven, CT: Yale University Press, 2011).

4. Steve Lohr, "Even a Giant Can Learn to Run," *New York Times*, December 31, 2011, accessed May 13, 2012, http://www .nytimes.com/2012/01/01/business/how-samuel-palmisano-of-ibm-stayed-a-step-ahead-unboxed.html.

5. *New York Times* science columnist John Tierney wrote a concise article on decision fatigue. See "Do You Suffer from Decision Fatigue?," *New York Times*, August 17, 2011, accessed June 28, 2012, http://www.nytimes.com/2011/08/21/magazine/do-you-suffer-from-decision-fatigue.html. For a more detailed explanation of decision fatigue and how the loss of willpower (ego depletion) affects self-control, see Roy Baumeister and John Tierney, *Willpower: Rediscovering the Greatest Human Strength* (New York: Penguin Press, 2011).

Chapter 9 – "Predict Your Fail Points"

1. If you've never done scenario planning or want to do it better, a good resource is Thomas Chermack, *Scenario Planning in Organizations: How to Create, Use, and Assess Scenarios* (San Francisco: Berrett-Koehler Publishers, 2011). His performance-based model looks at planning as a system that lays out alternative road maps when conditions are ambiguous or uncertain, a perfect place to fold in consideration of fail points that traditional strategic planning processes may overlook.

Chapter 11 – "Fail Early, Often, and Smart"

1. Eric Ries, *The Lean Startup: How Today's Entrepreneurs Use Continuous Innovation to Create Radically Successful Businesses* (New York: Crown Business, 2011).

Chapter 12 – "Build Learning into Everything"

1. Chris Argyris, "Teaching Smart People How to Learn," *Harvard Business Review* 69, no. 3 (May-June 1991): 99–109.
2. For a description of the Afterburner program that the New York Giants went through, see James D. Murphy, *Flawless Execution: Use the Techniques and Systems of America's Fighter Pilots to Perform at Your Peak and Win the Battles of the Business World* (New York: Harper Business, 2006). Chapter 15 covers debriefing.
3. Damon Hack, "One Giant Leap for Manningkind," *Sports Illustrated*, February 13, 2012.
4. Marilyn Darling, Charles Parry, and Joseph Moore explain how the army's after-action review process focuses on learning from lessons, not just lessons learned, in "Learning in the

Thick of It," *Harvard Business Review* 83, no. 7 (July-August 2005): 84–92, 192.

Chapter 15 – "Have the Tough Conversations"

1. Since knowing how to have effective tough conversations doesn't come naturally to most of us, I recommend these two books on the topic. Both cover the fundamental issues that keep us dropping the ball on important conversations or avoiding them altogether. Each lays out a strategy to turn anger, hurt, and frustration into honest dialogue and improved relationships.

   Douglas Stone, Bruce Patton, and Sheila Heen are associated with the Harvard Law School and the Harvard Project on Negotiation. In *Difficult Conversations: How to Discuss What Matters Most*, rev. ed. (New York: Penguin Group, 2010), they see a tough conversation as actually being three different conversations: what happened, feelings, and identity. While not easy or quick, their model shows you how to move around effectively in each conversation and pull them all together.

   In *Crucial Conversations: Tools for Talking When Stakes Are High*, 2nd ed. (New York: McGraw-Hill, 2011), authors Kerry Patterson, Joseph Grenny, Ron McMillan, and Al Switzler define tough conversations as those with high stakes, varied opinions, and strong emotions. They offer seven principles to improve dialogue skills, including how to talk, listen, and act together, and a contextual model to understand how it all fits.

2. An explanation of Chris Argyris's left-hand column exercise can be found in his article "Skilled Incompetence," *Harvard Business Review* 64, no. 5 (September 1986): 74–79.

   Another description of the left-hand column exercise is in "The Ladder of Inference," part of the "Mental Models" section in Peter M. Senge, Charlotte Roberts, Richard B. Ross, Bryan J. Smith, and Art Kleiner, *The Fifth Discipline Fieldbook: Strategies and Tools for Building a Learning Organization* (New York: Currency Doubleday, 1994), 246–252.

3. Senge et al. also describe "Balancing Advocacy and Inquiry" in the "Mental Models" section of *The Fifth Discipline Fieldbook*, 253–259. If you're unfamiliar with the principles and practices

of the learning organization, this book is the pragmatic place to start.

Chapter 16 – "Supporting Smart Risk Taking"

1. The criteria for Tata Innovista's annual innovation awards can be found at these links, accessed June 26, 2012:
   http://www.tatainnovista.com/DTT.htm
   http://www.tatainnovista.com/TLE.htm
   http://www.tatainnovista.com/PI.htm

2. For an article profiling Kimberly-Clark's David Richter, see Lucas Merian, "Creating Culture of IT Innovation Includes Rewarding Failure," *Computerworld*, April 6, 2012, accessed June 26, 2012 at http://www.computerworld.com/s/article/9225870/Creating_culture_of_IT_innovation_includes_rewarding_failure.

INDEX